MW01195733

Lacy Sunshine's TM

The Great Adventures Of Eleanor and Pickles Coloring Book Volume 17

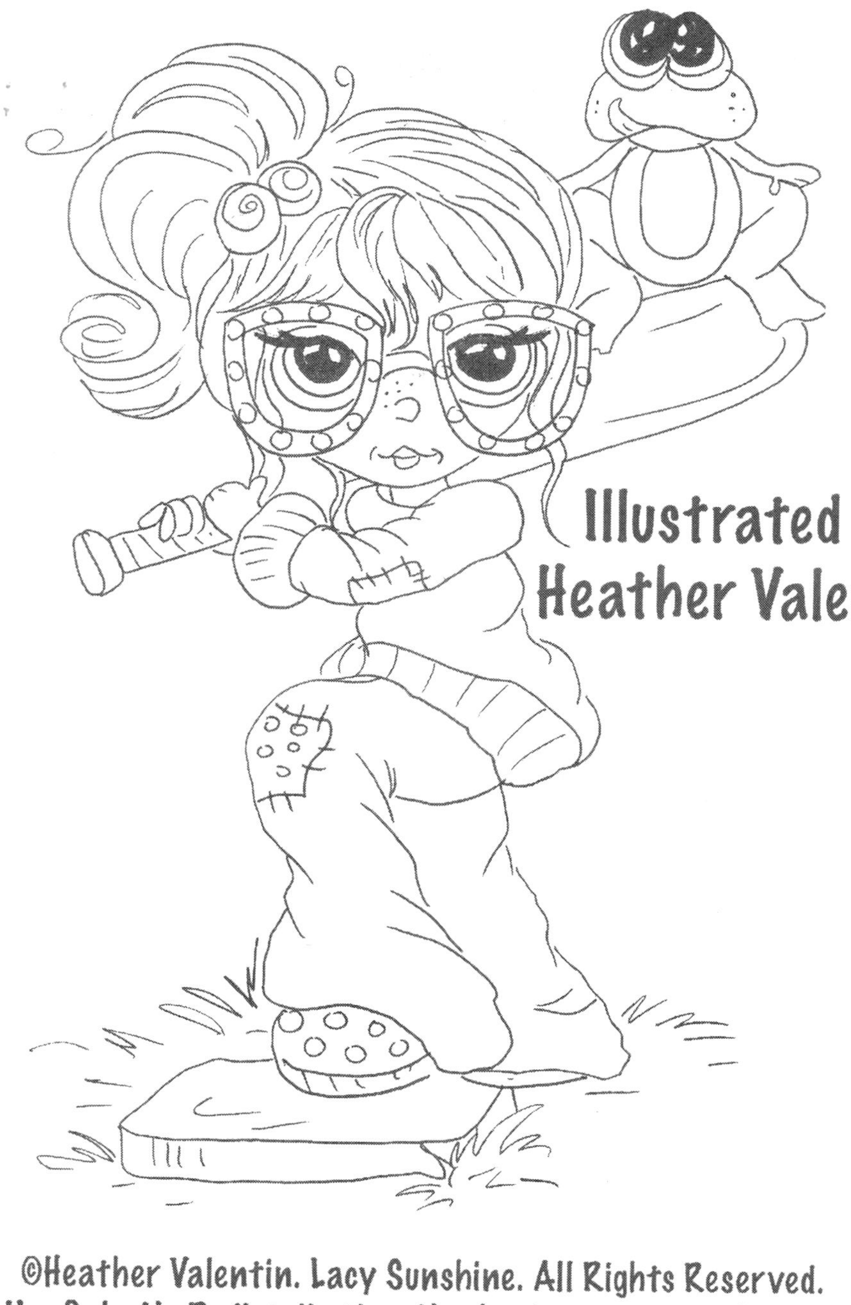

Illustrated by
Heather Valentin

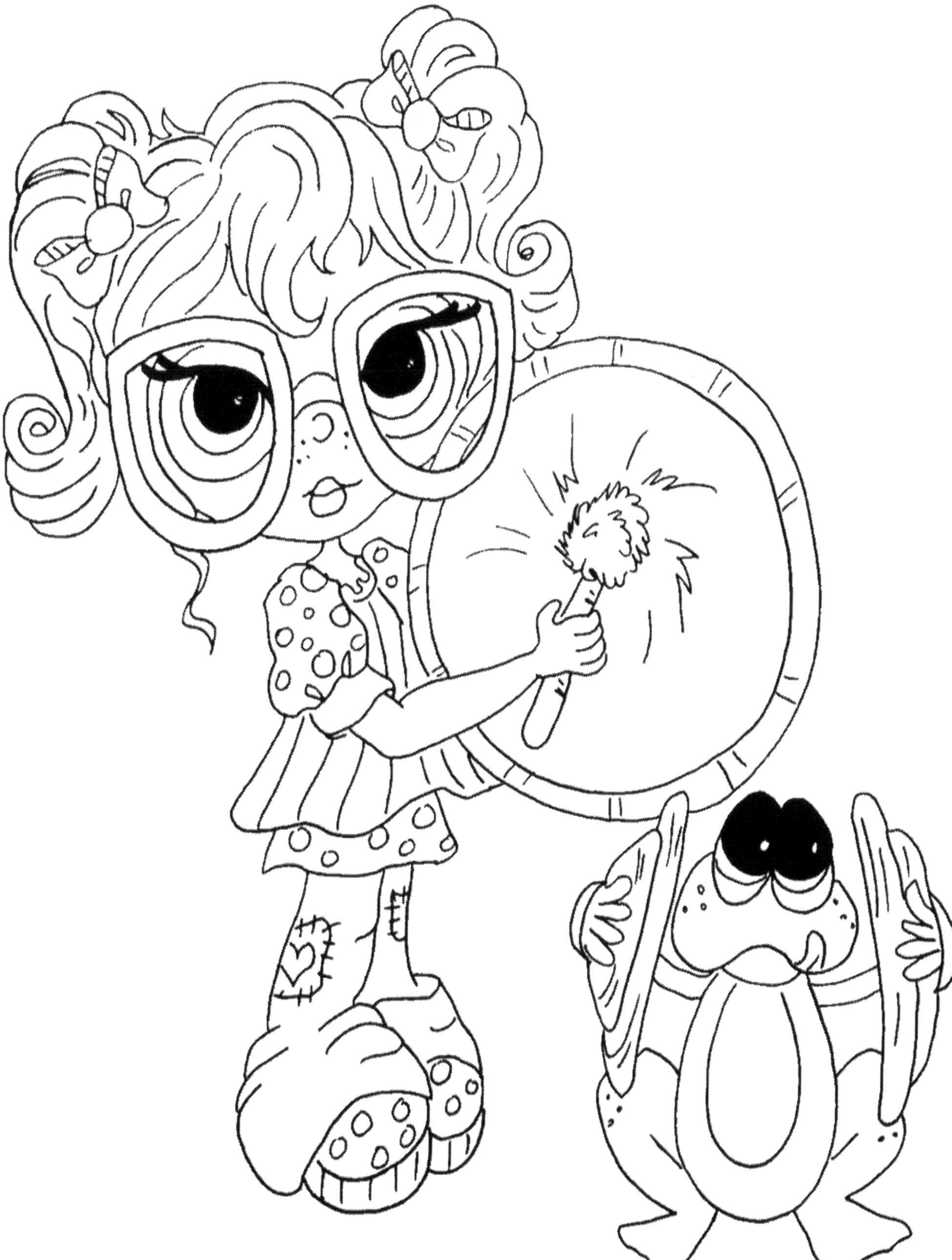

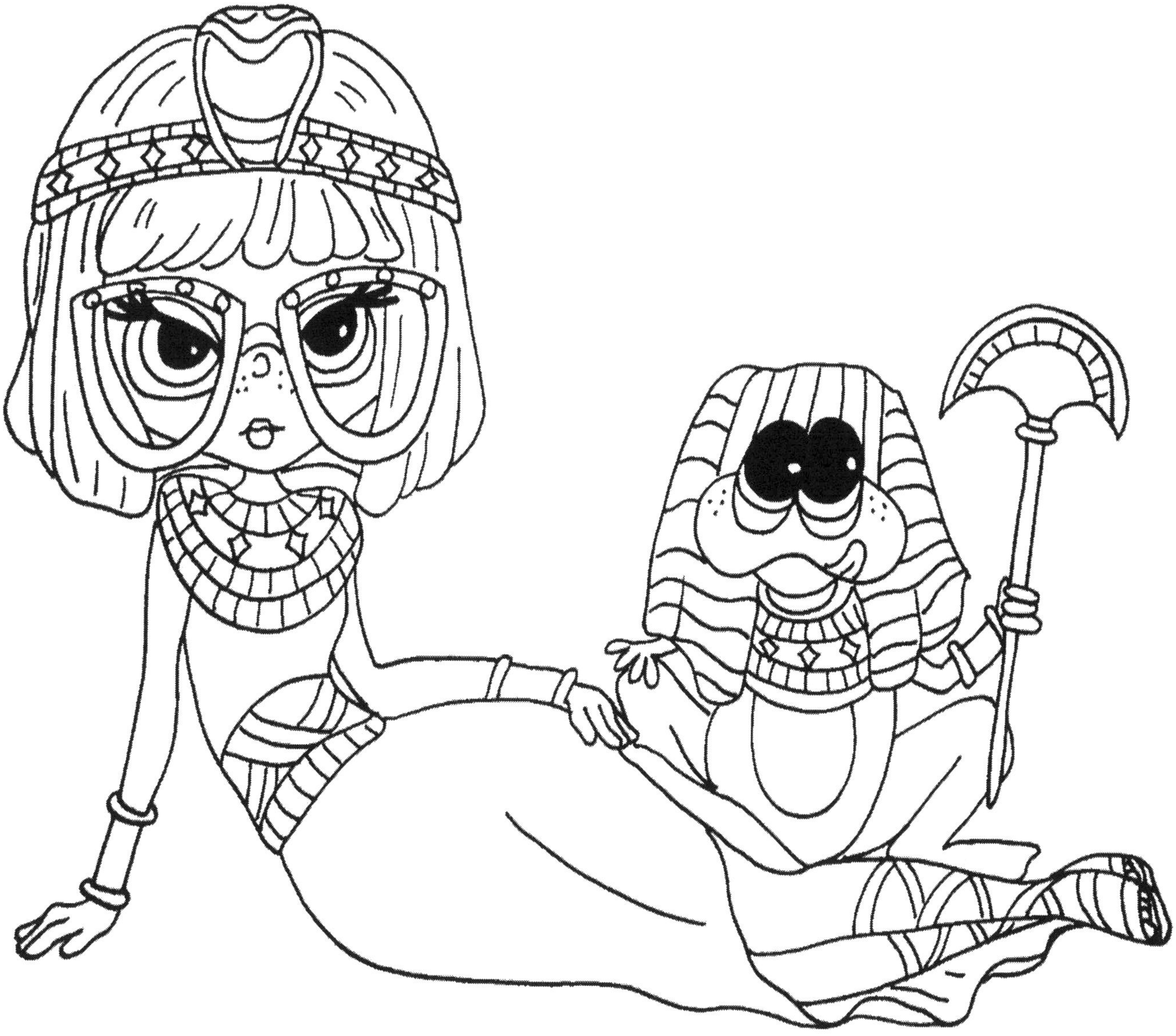

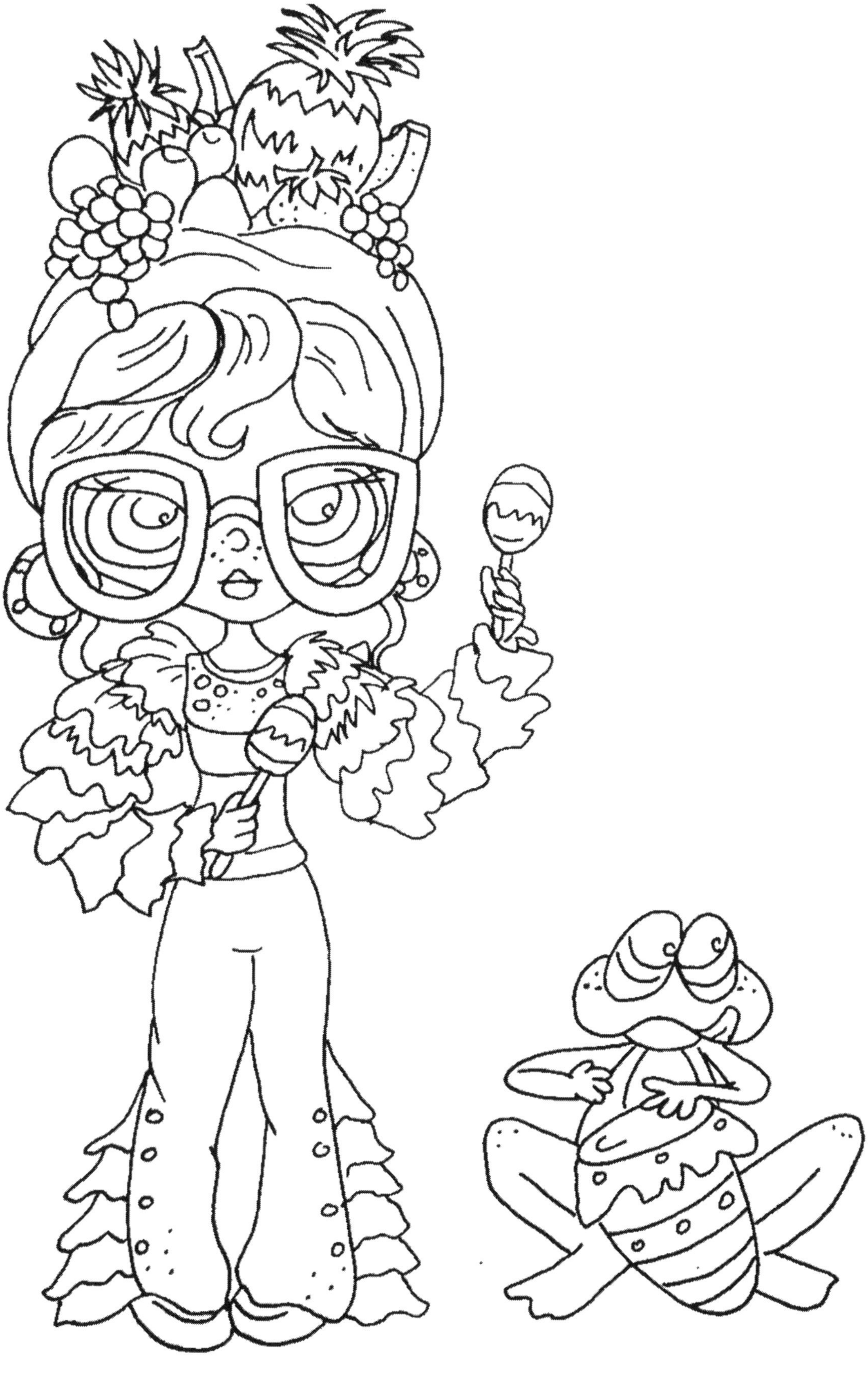

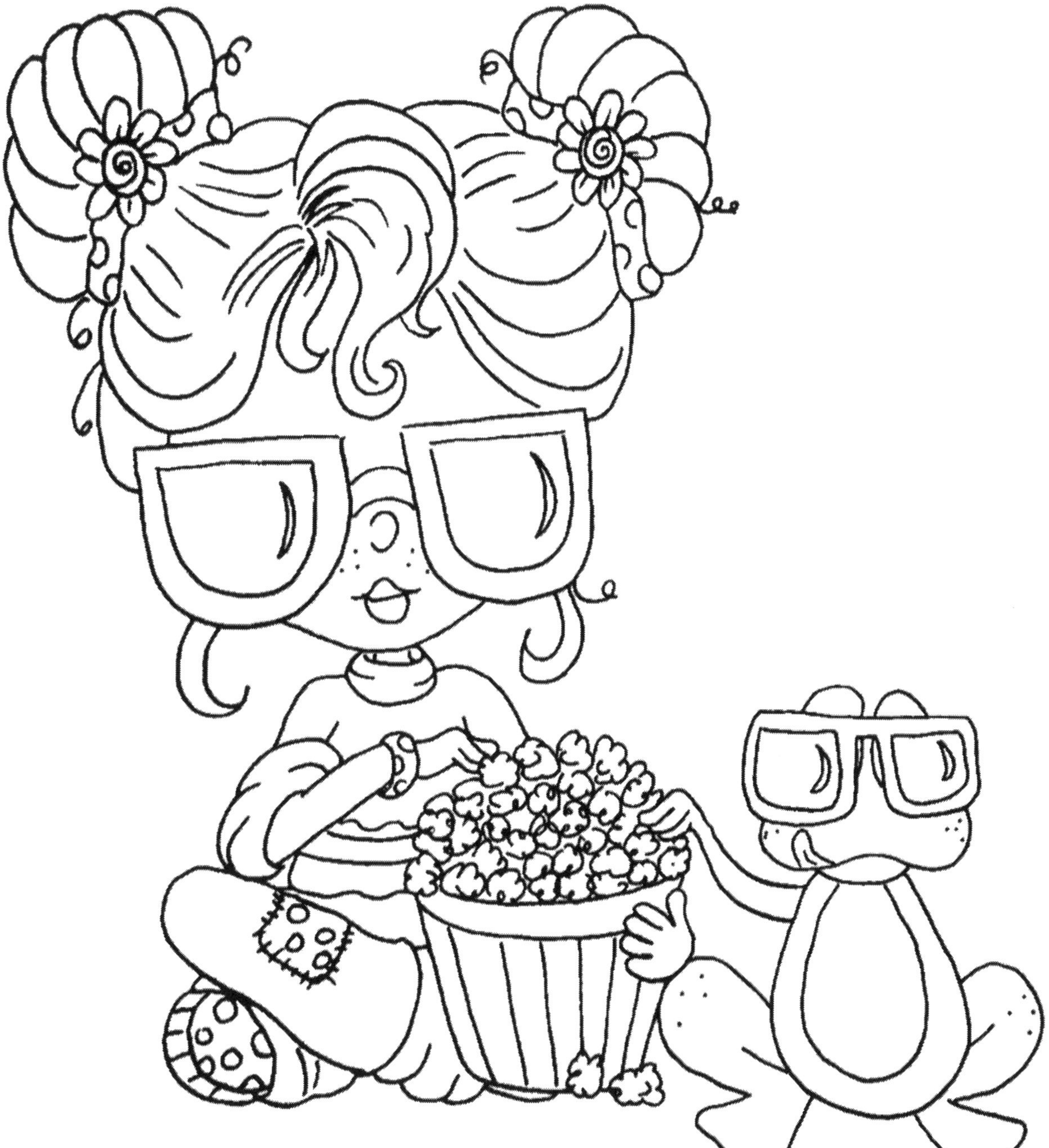

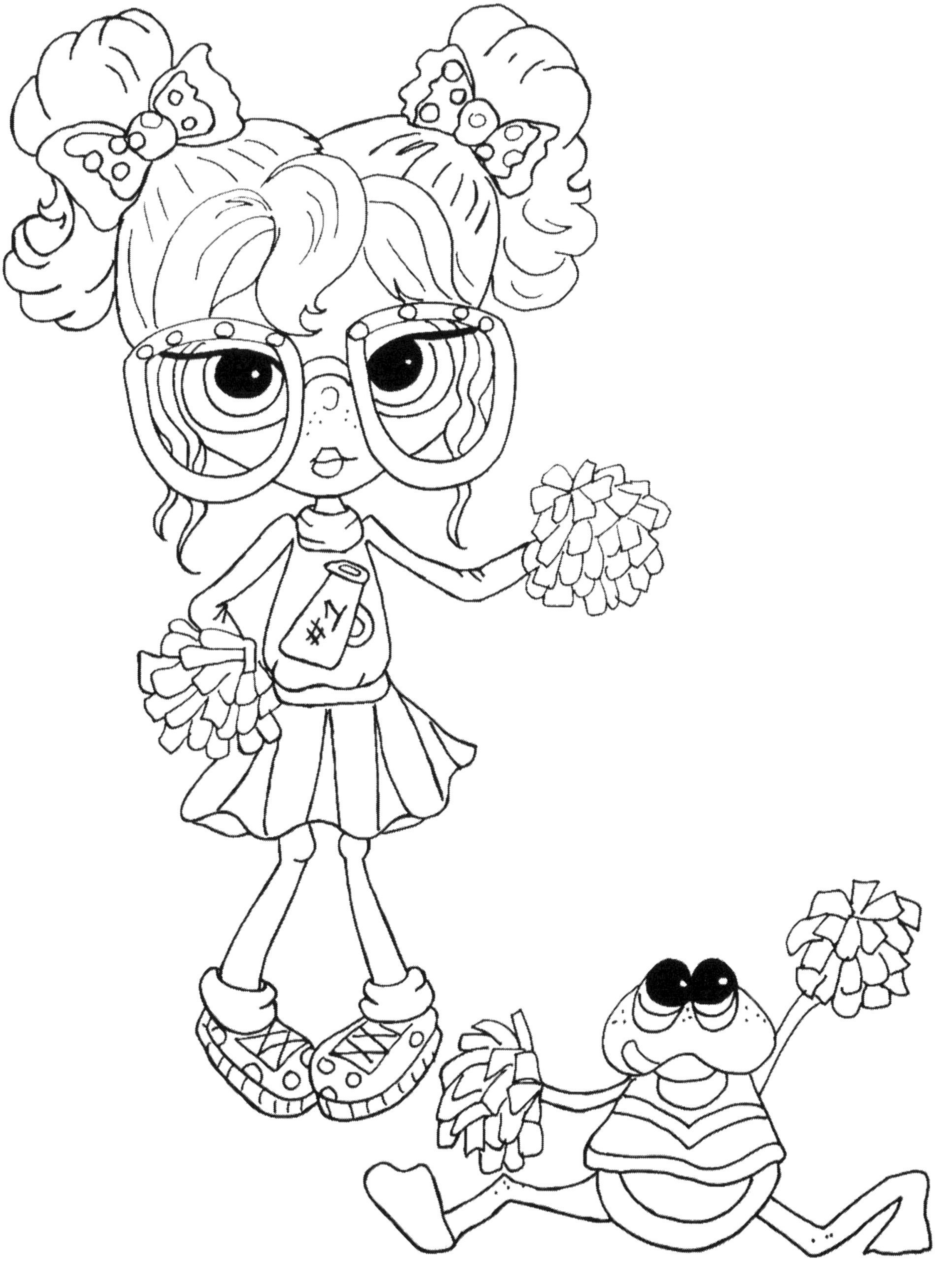
#1

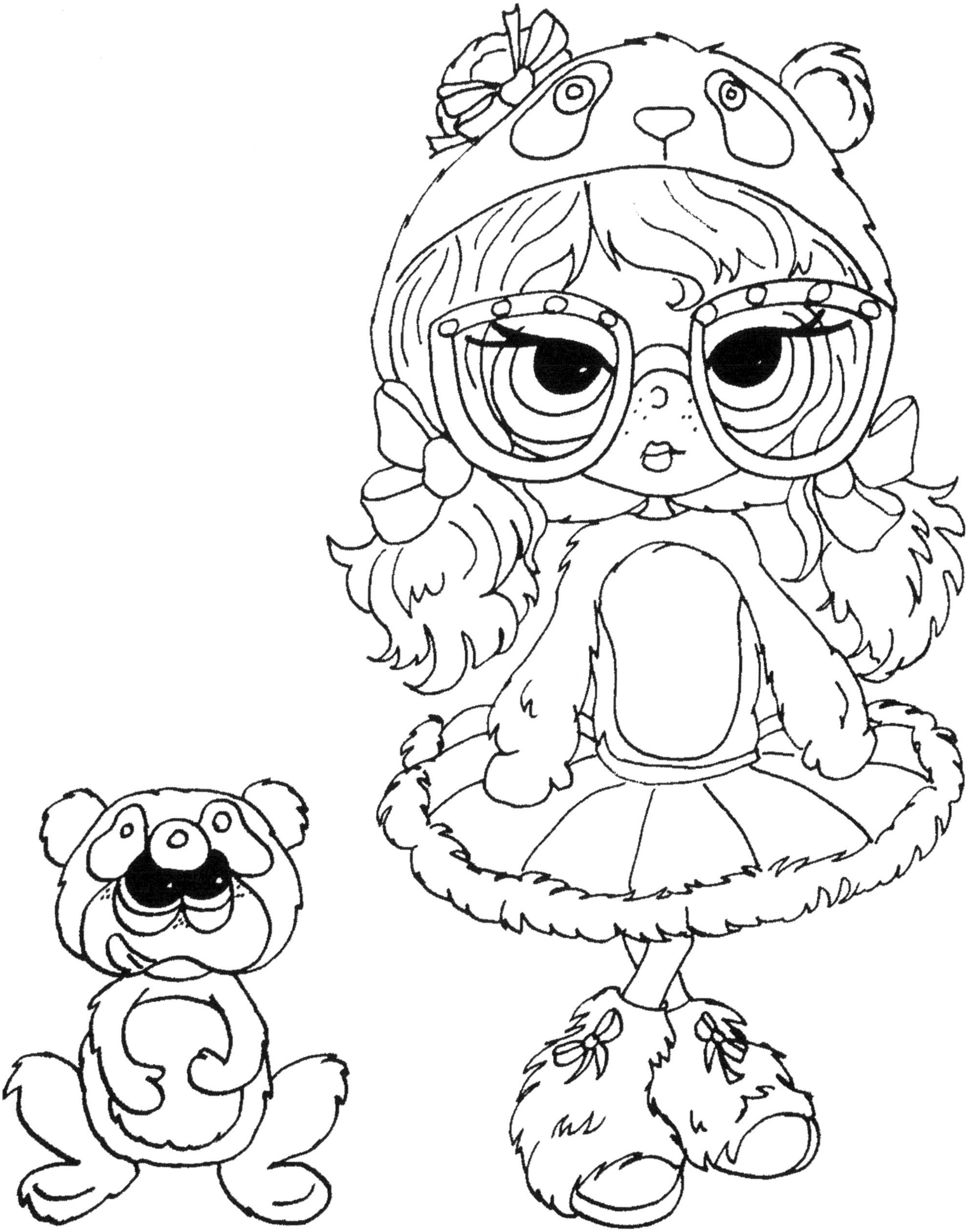

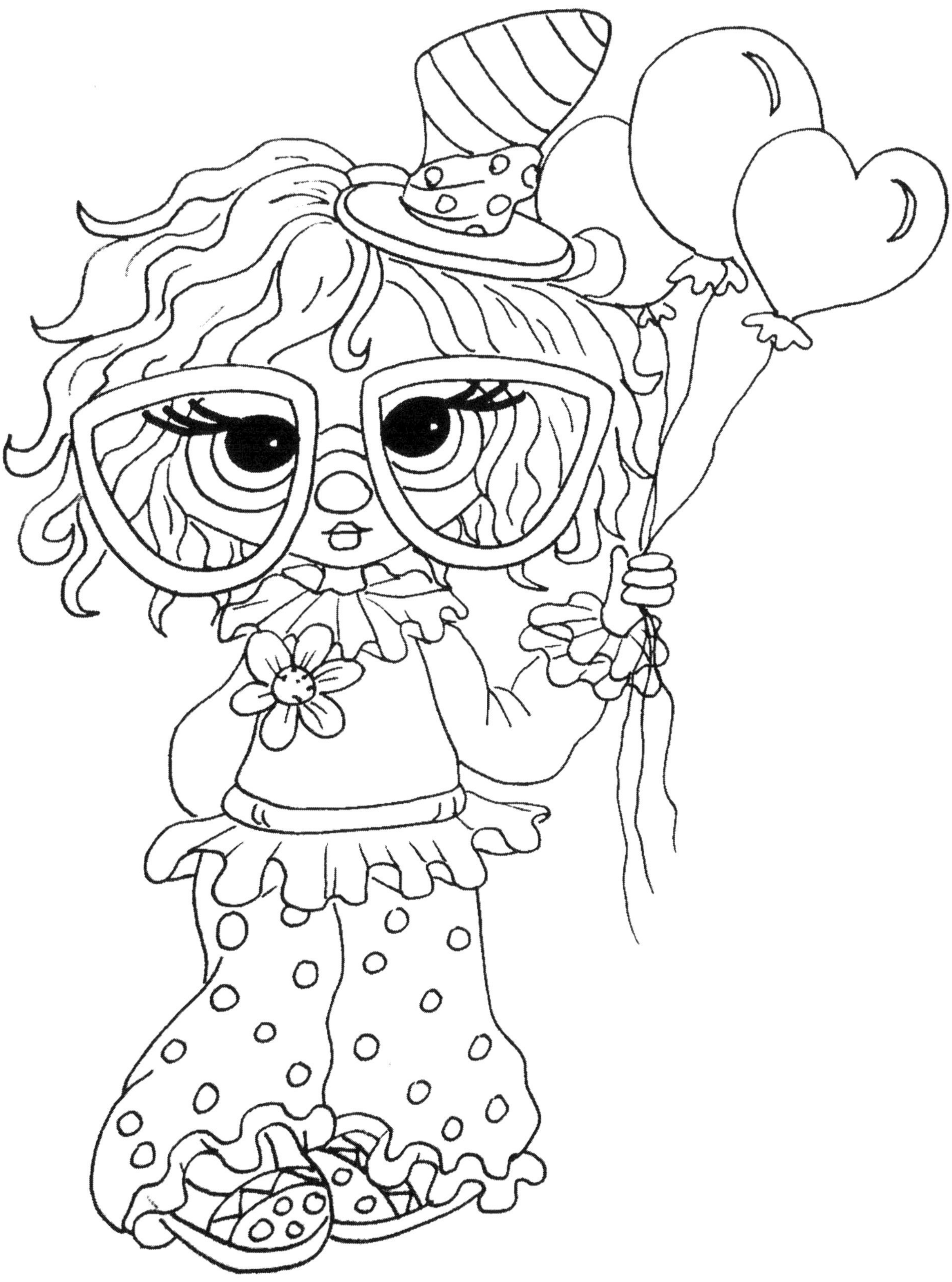

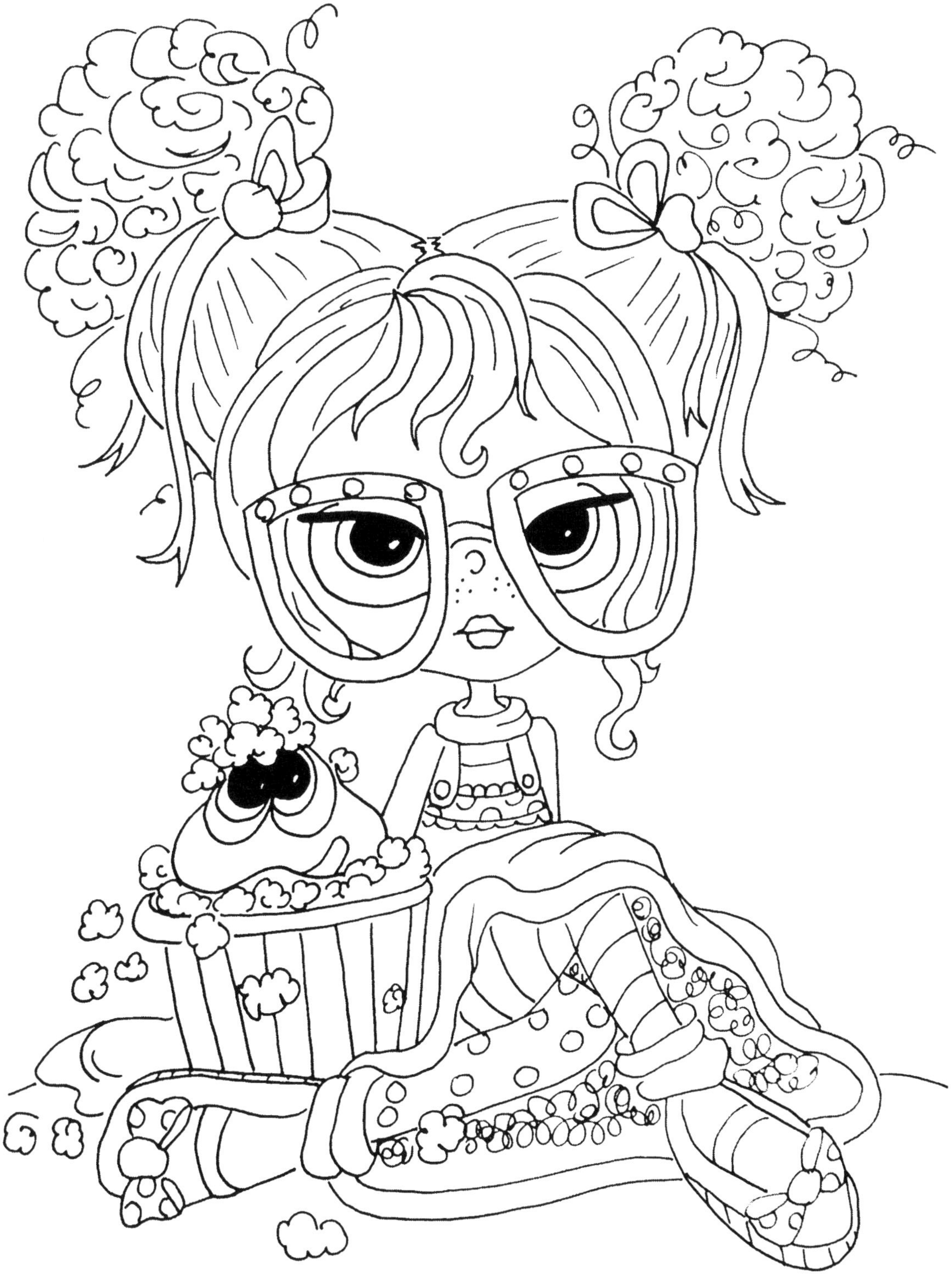

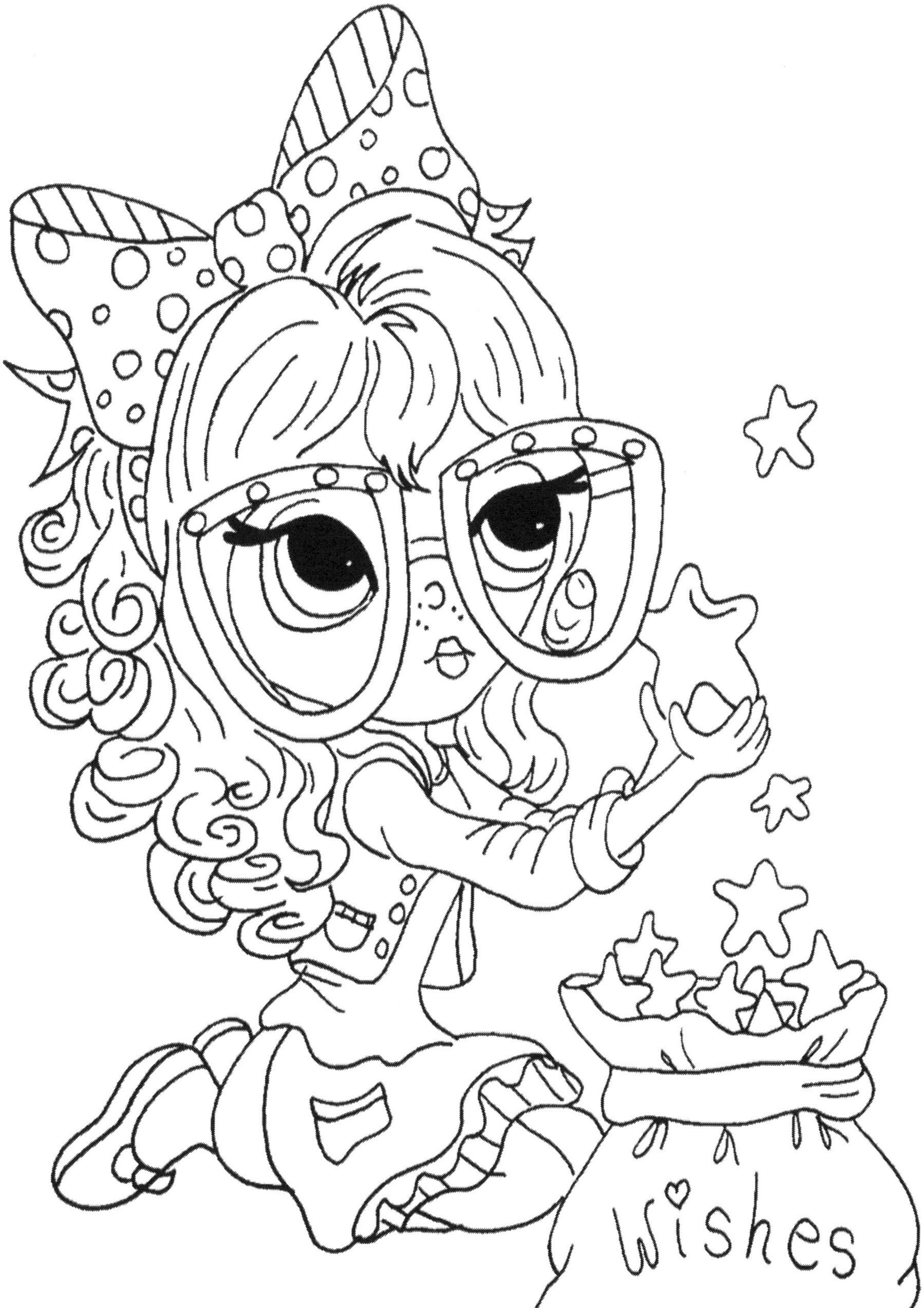
Wishes

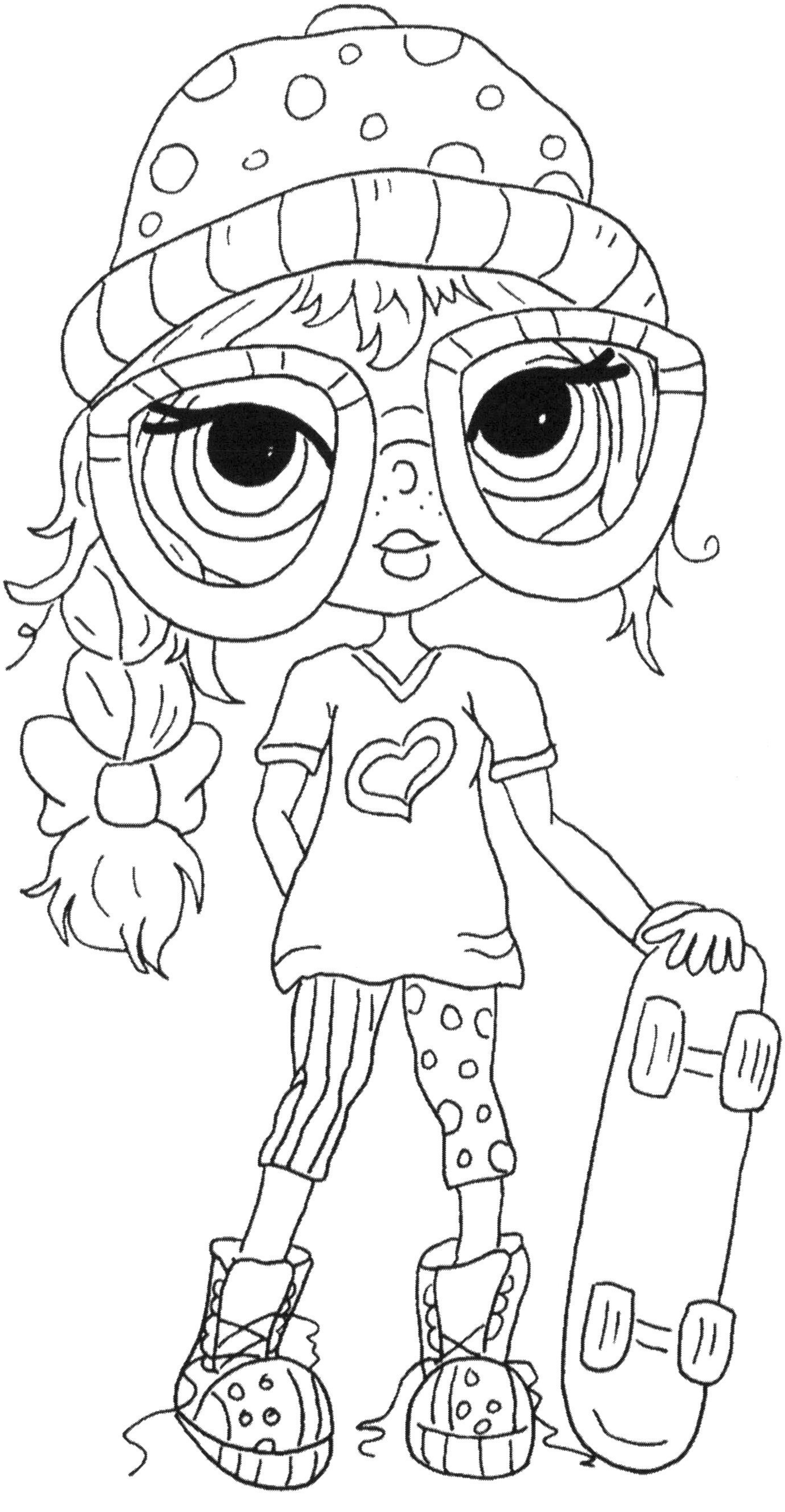

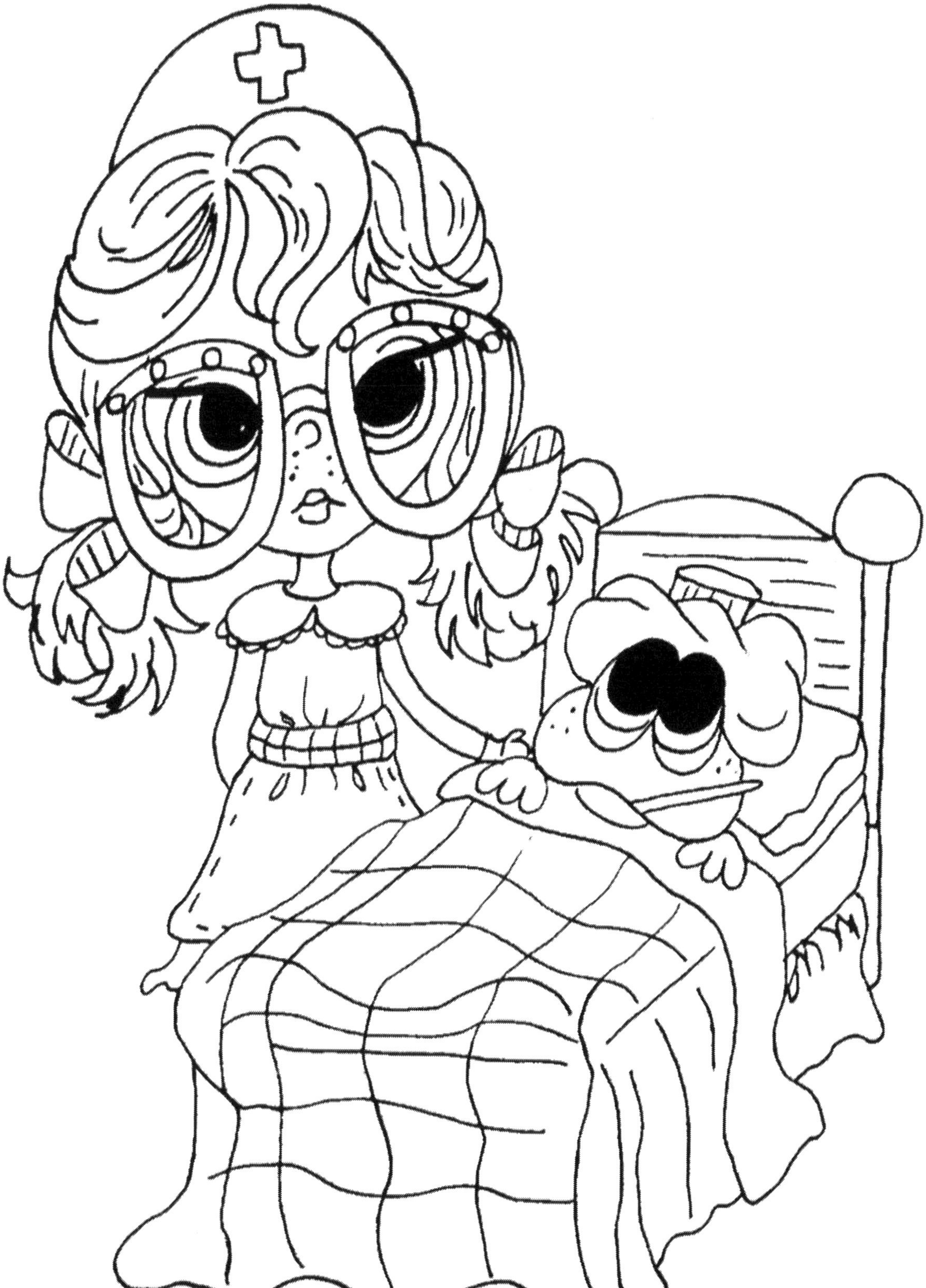

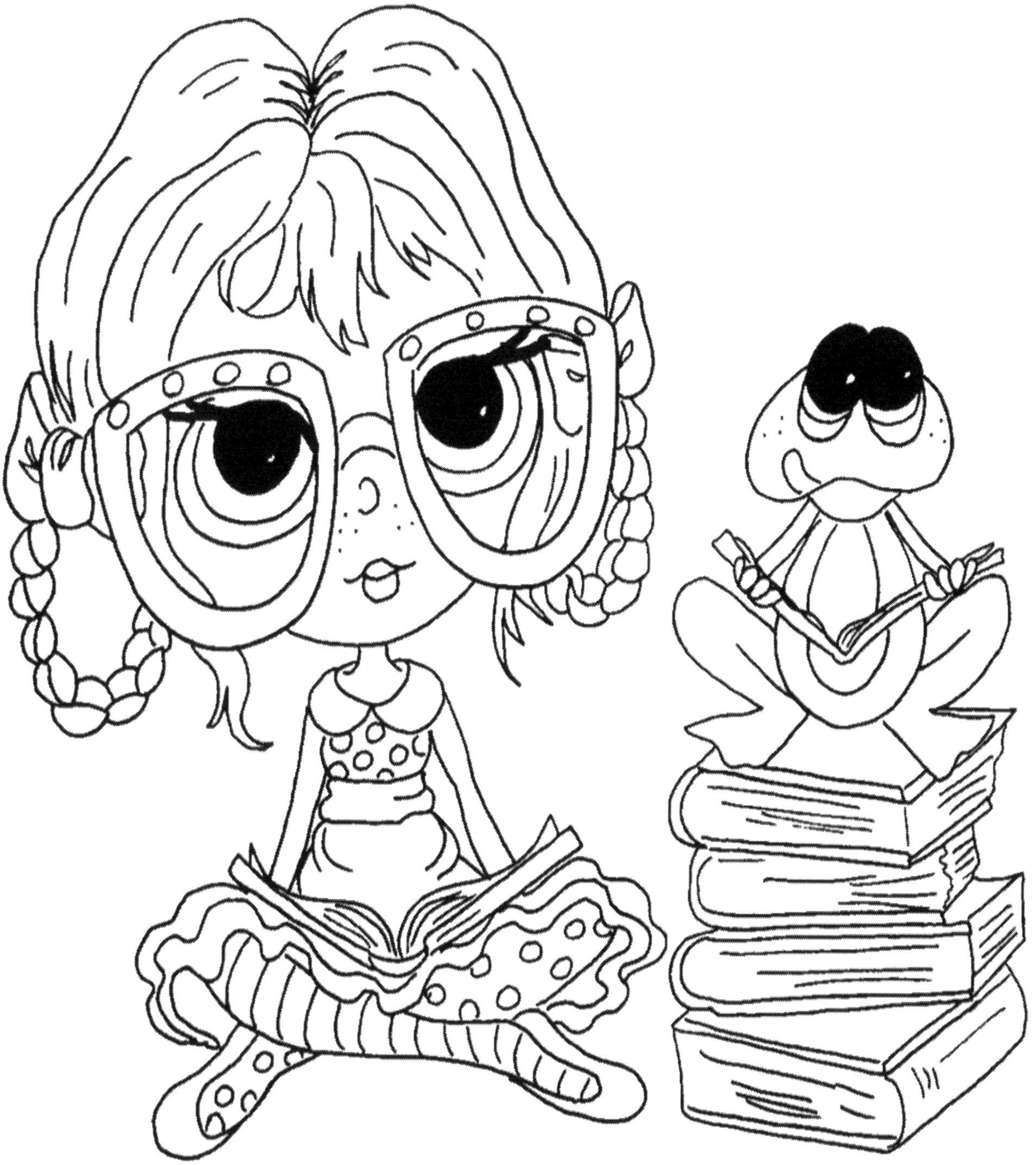

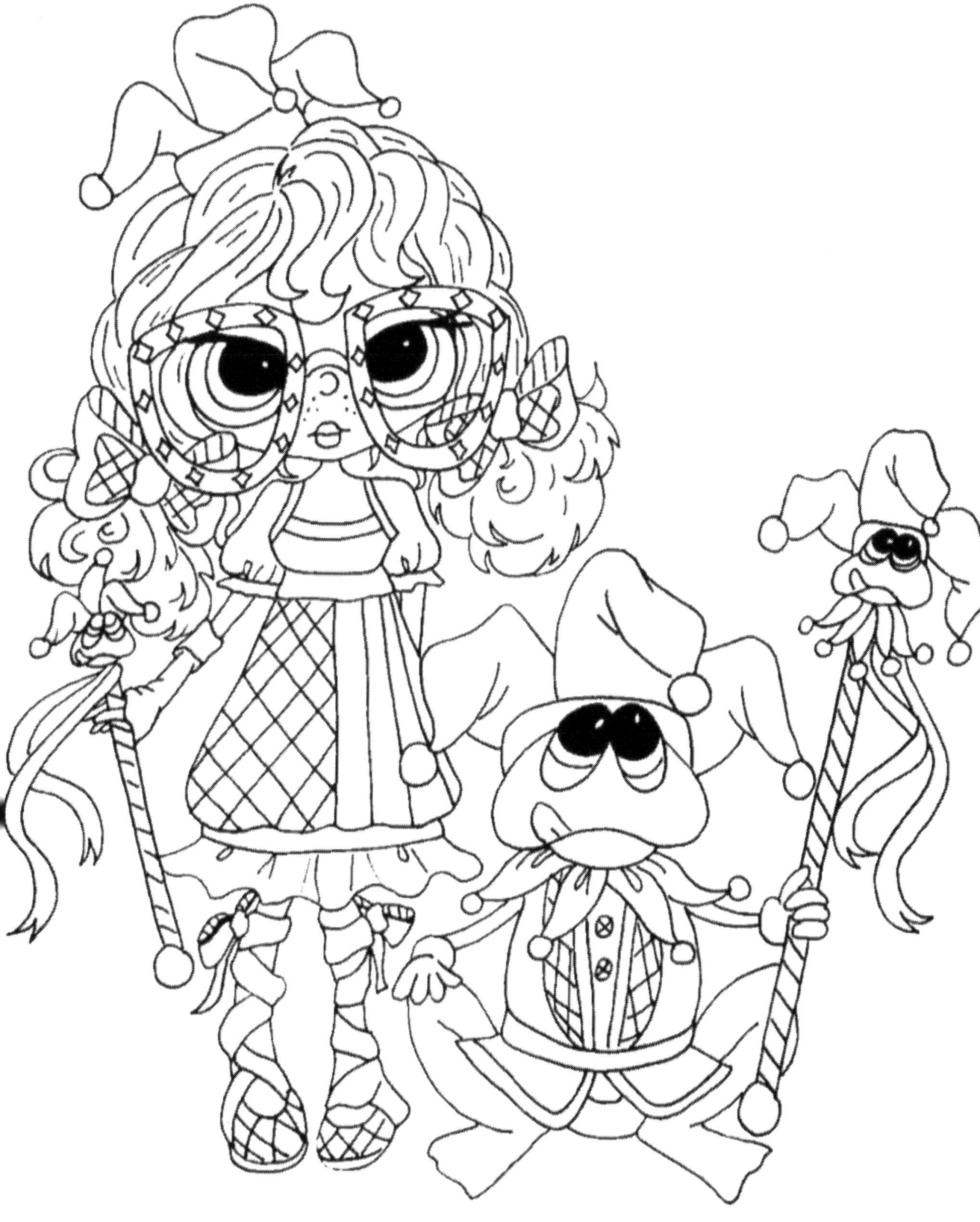

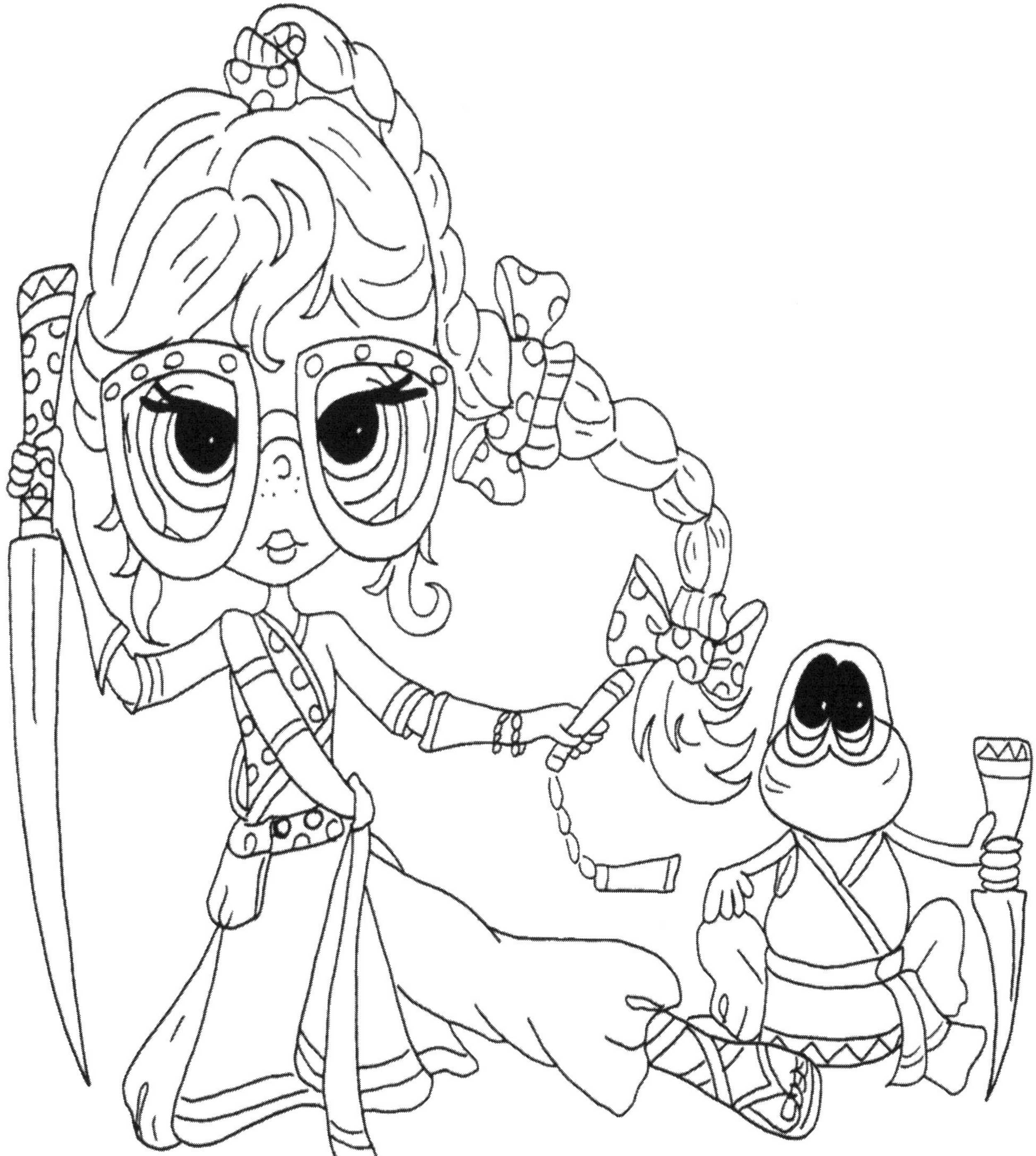

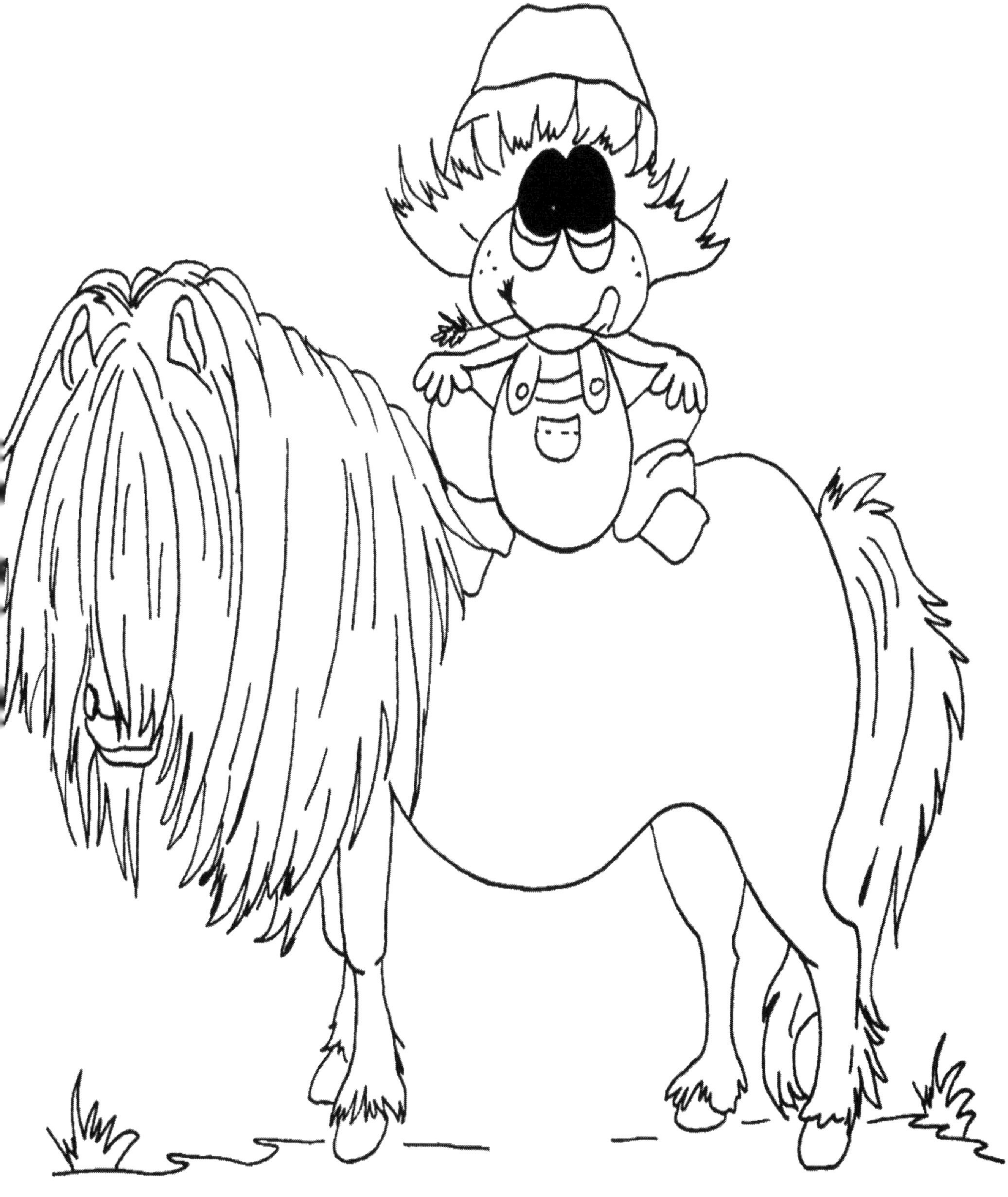

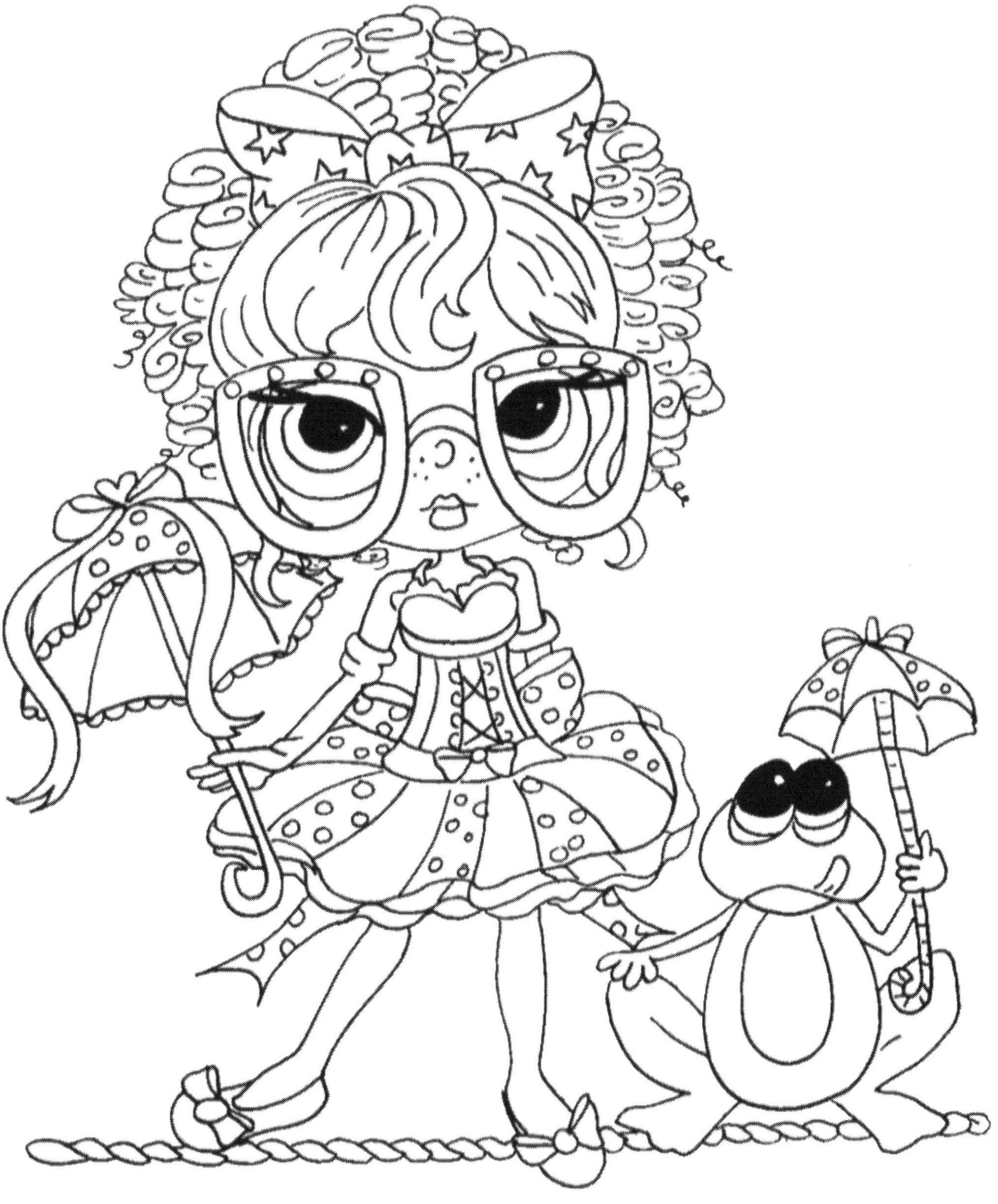

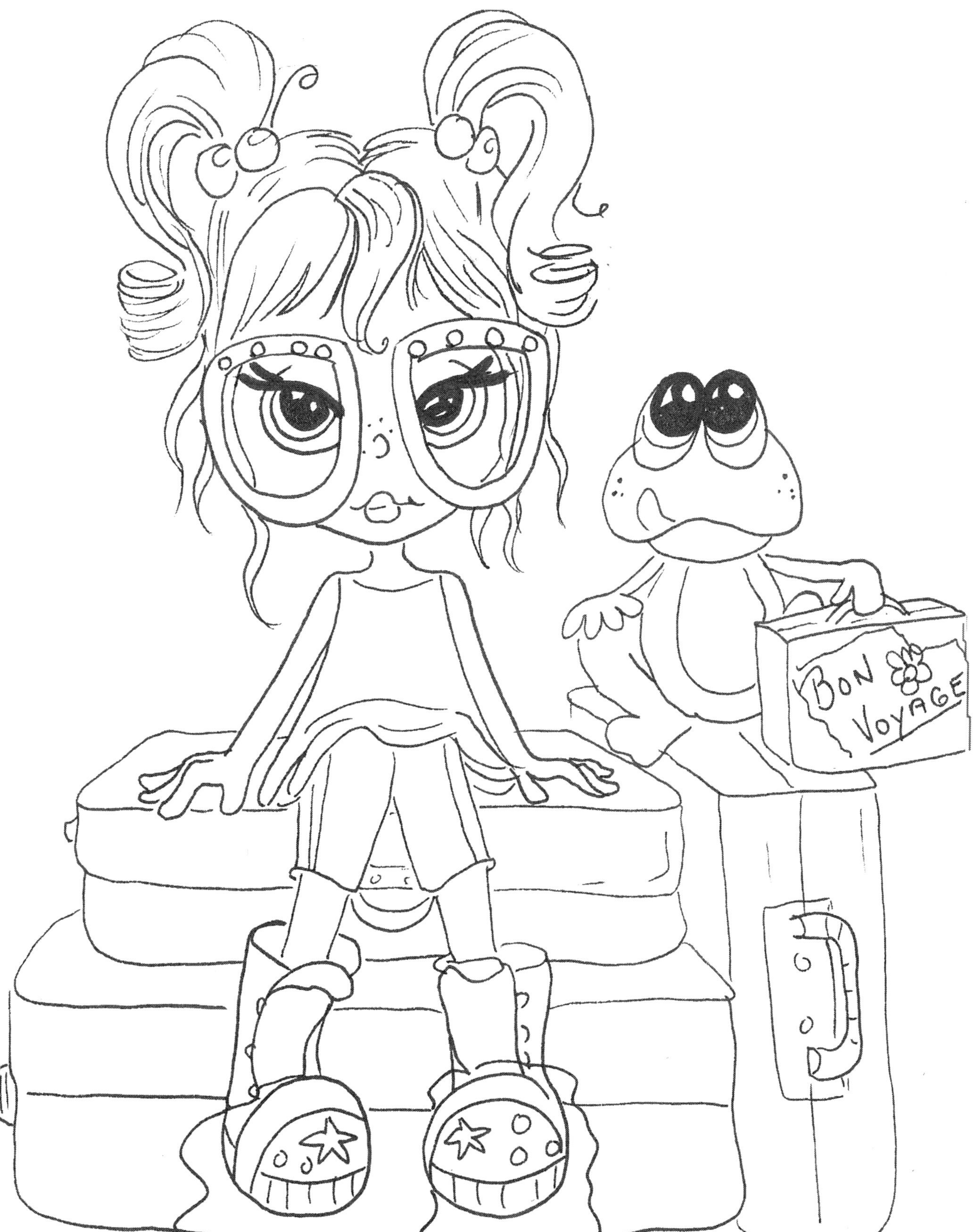
BON
VOYAGE

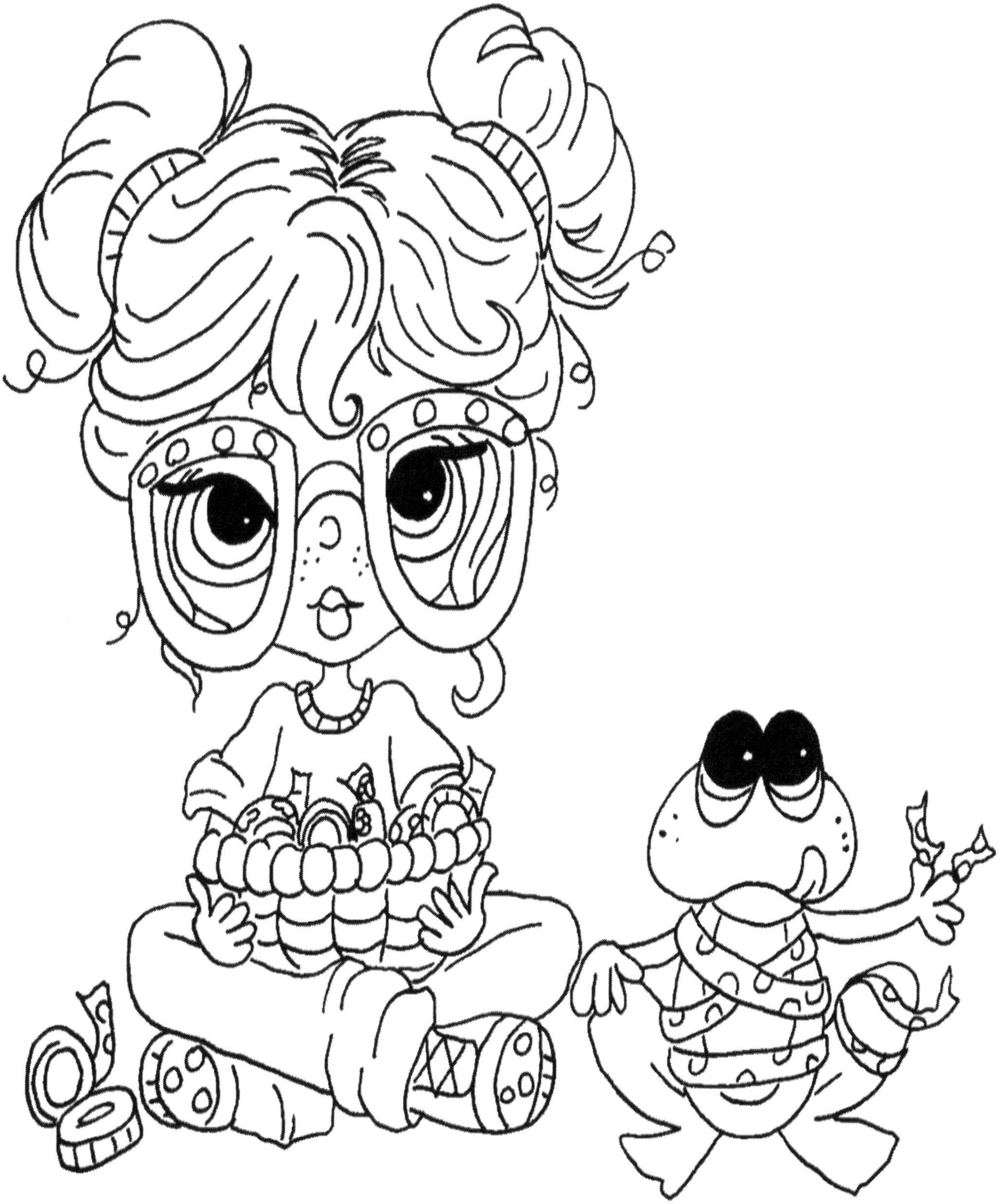

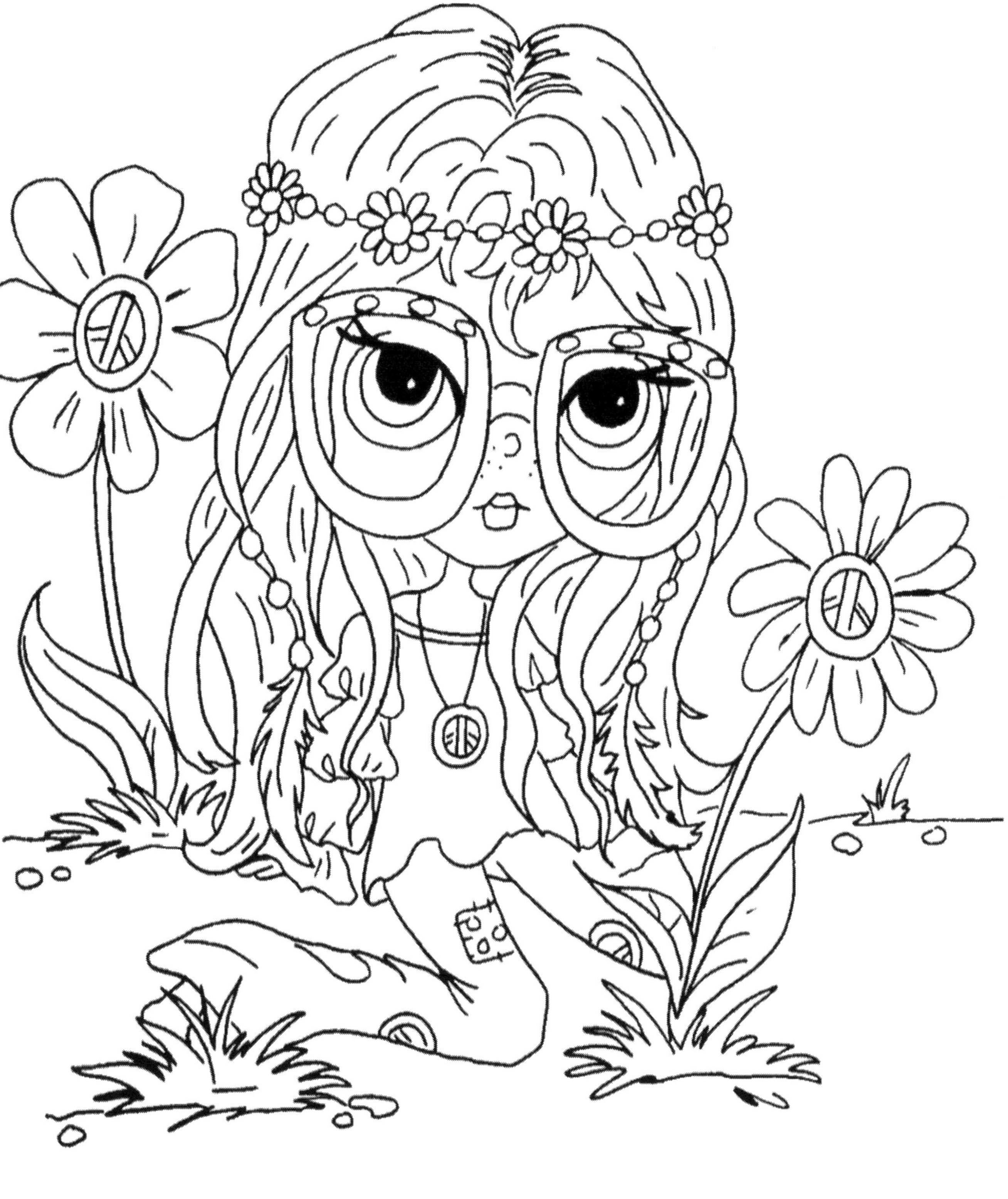

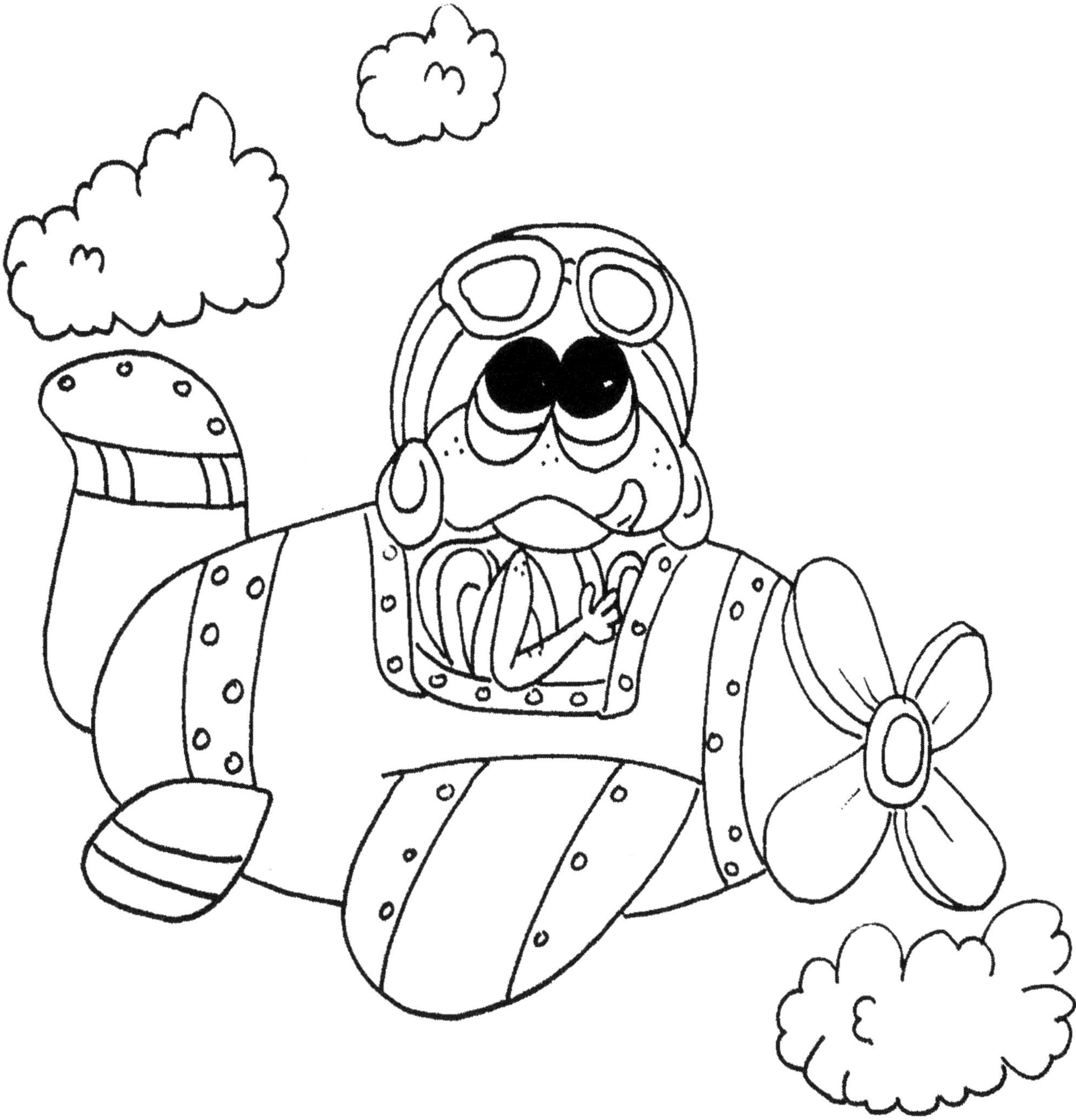

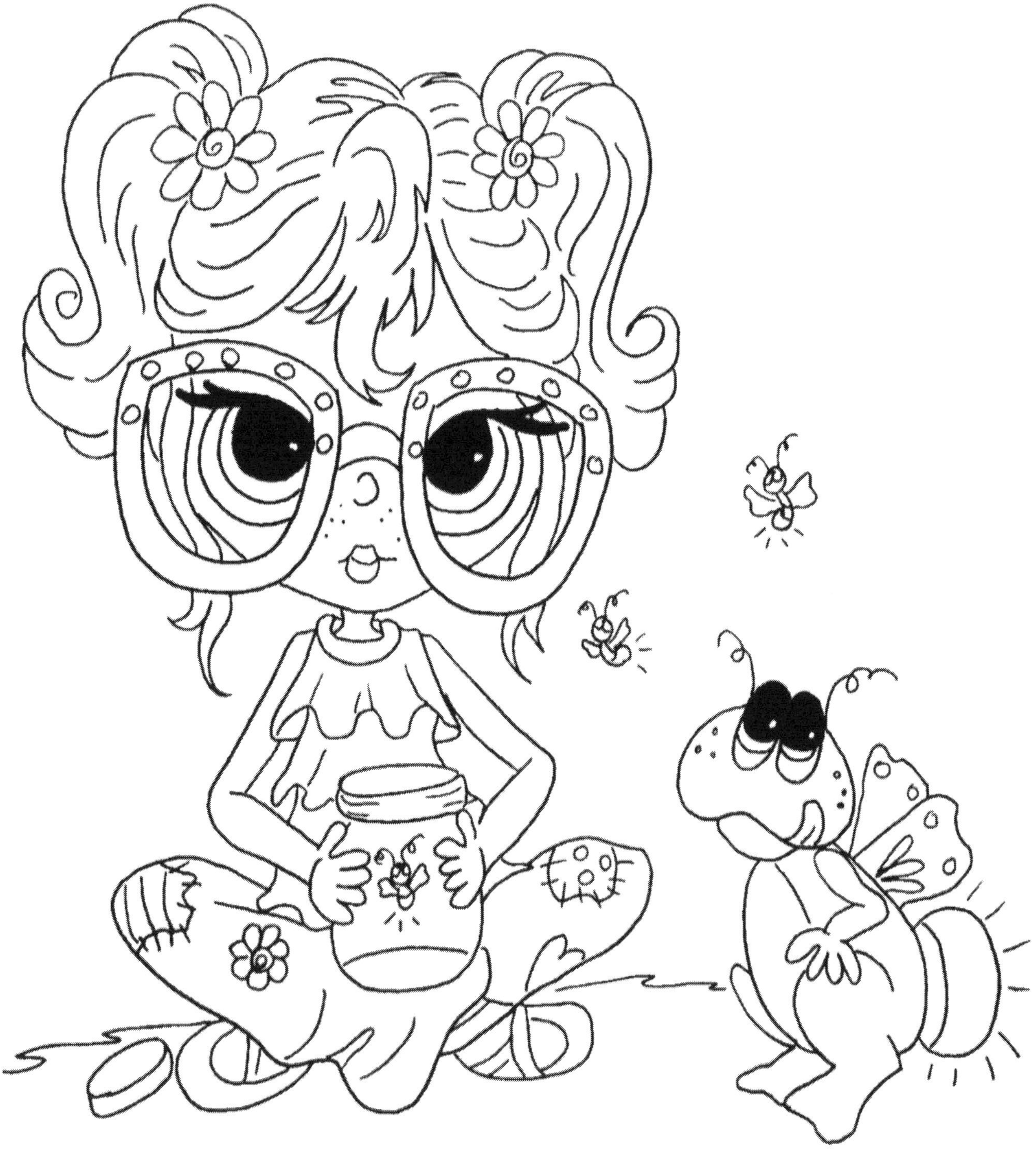

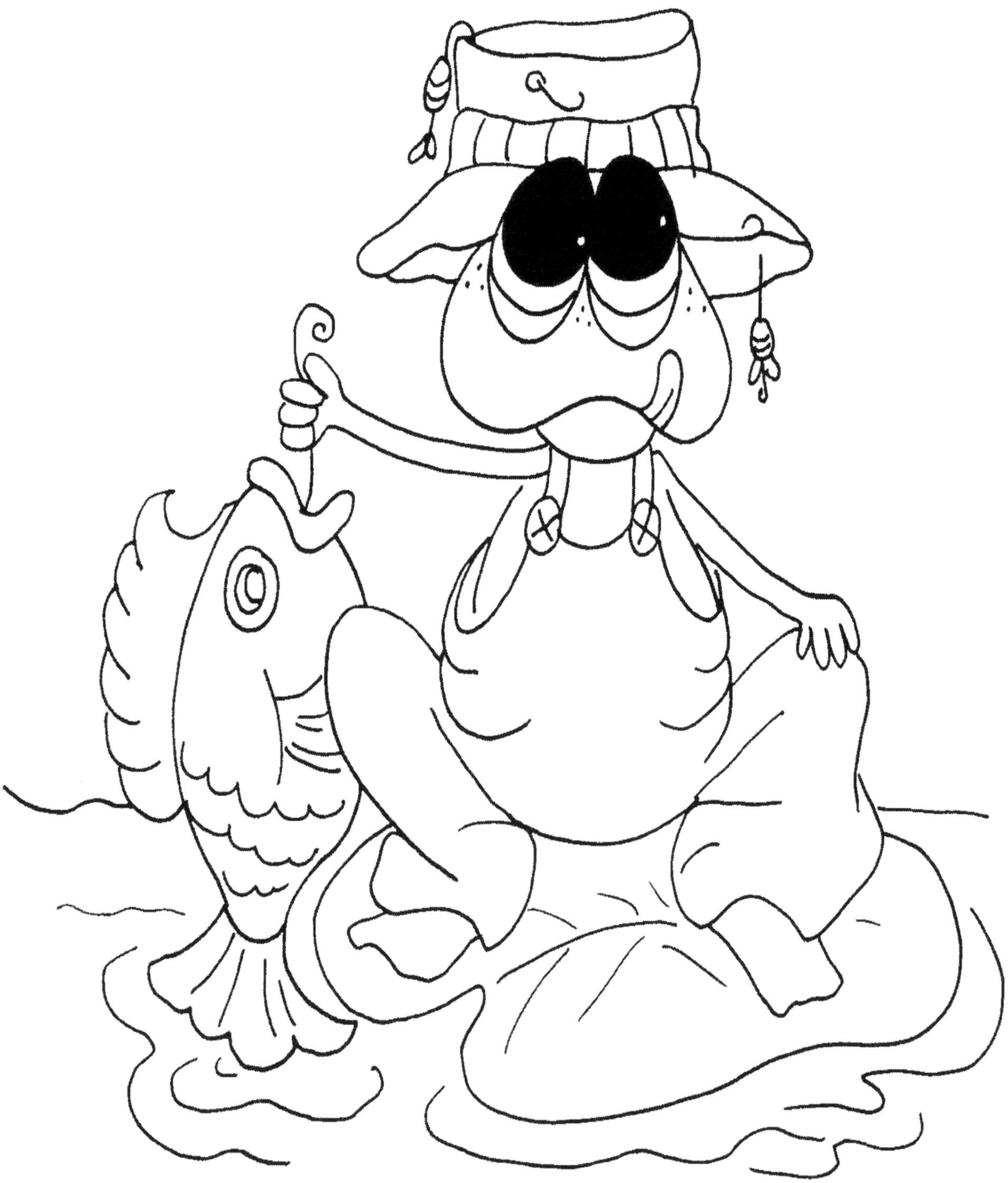

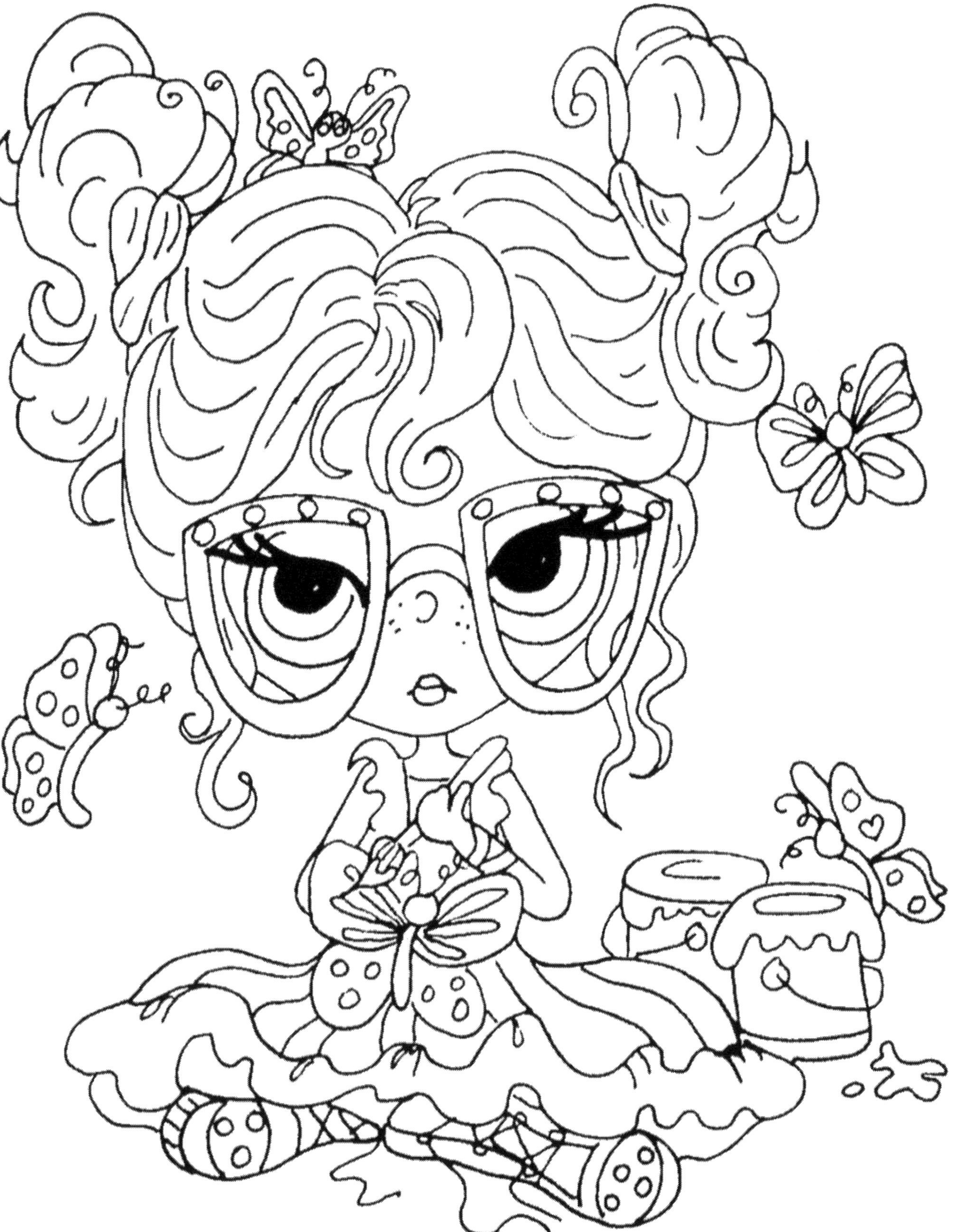

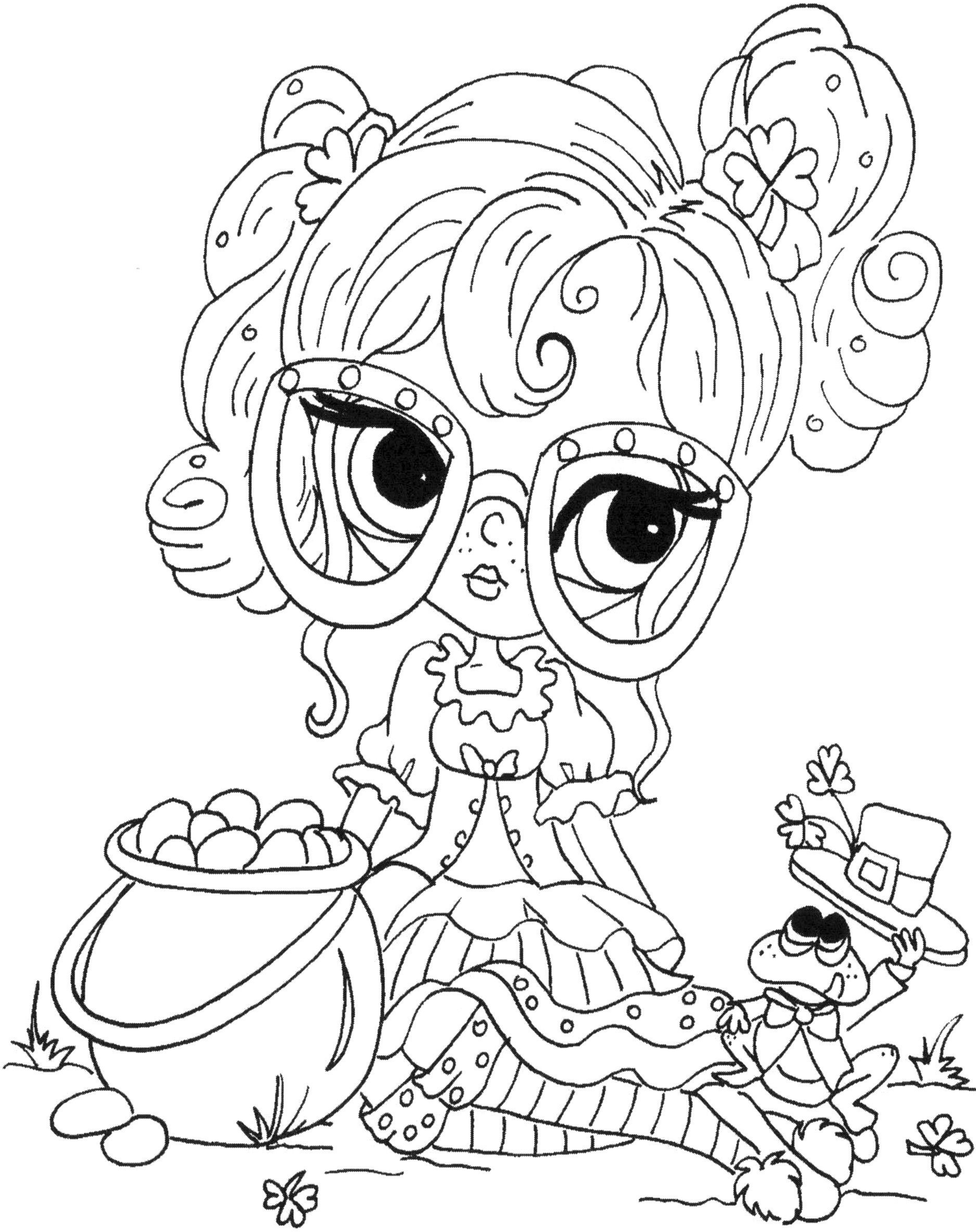

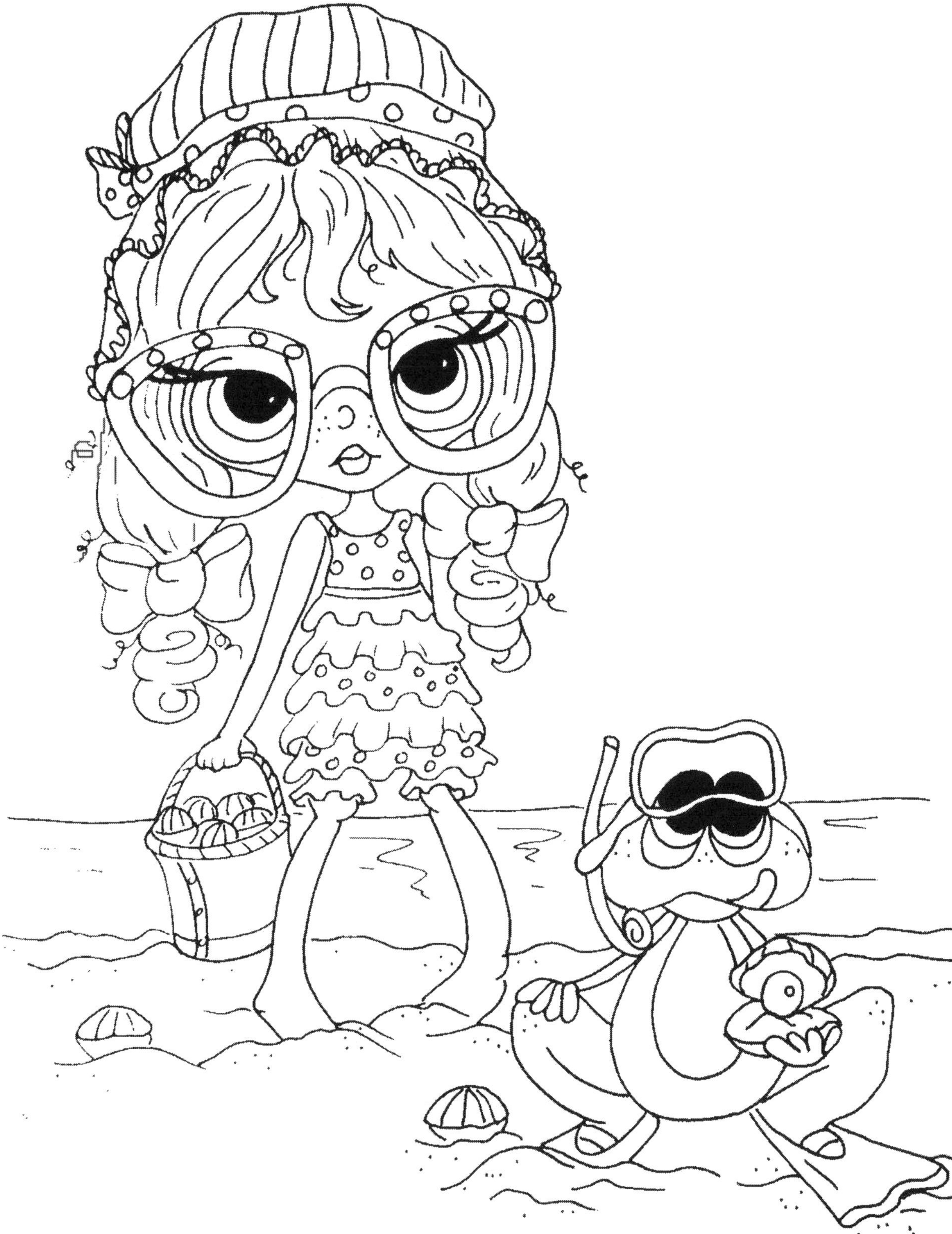

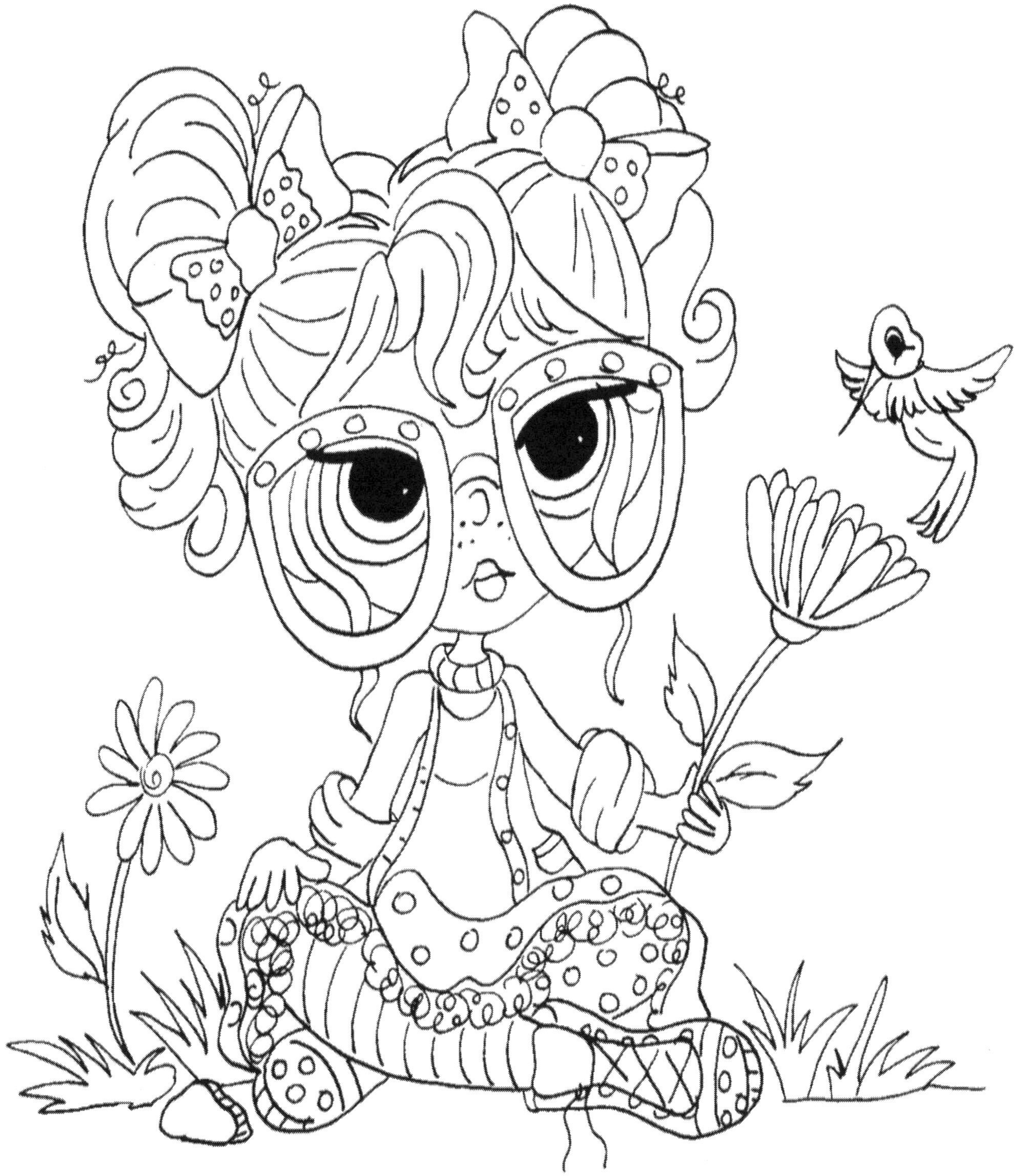

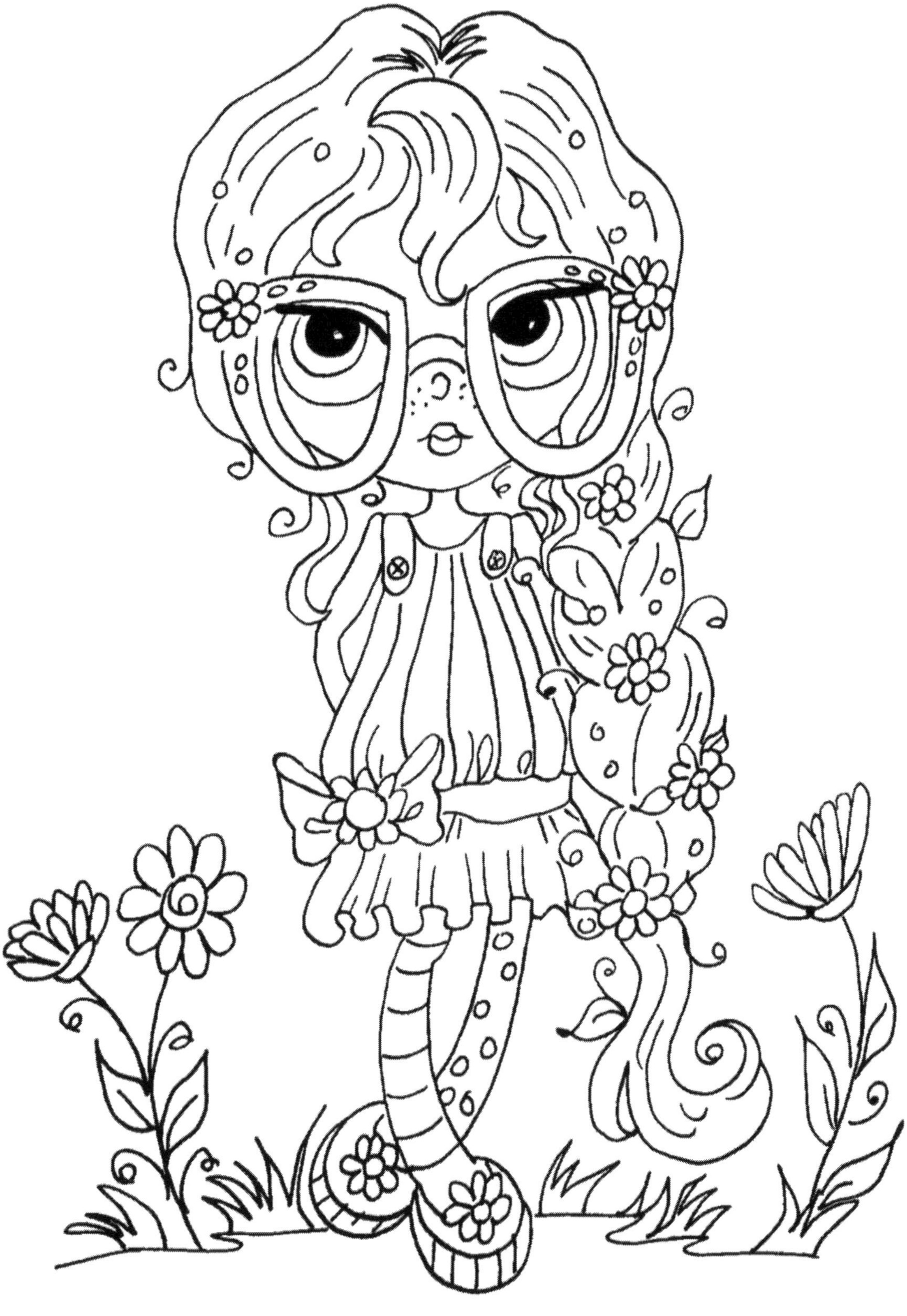

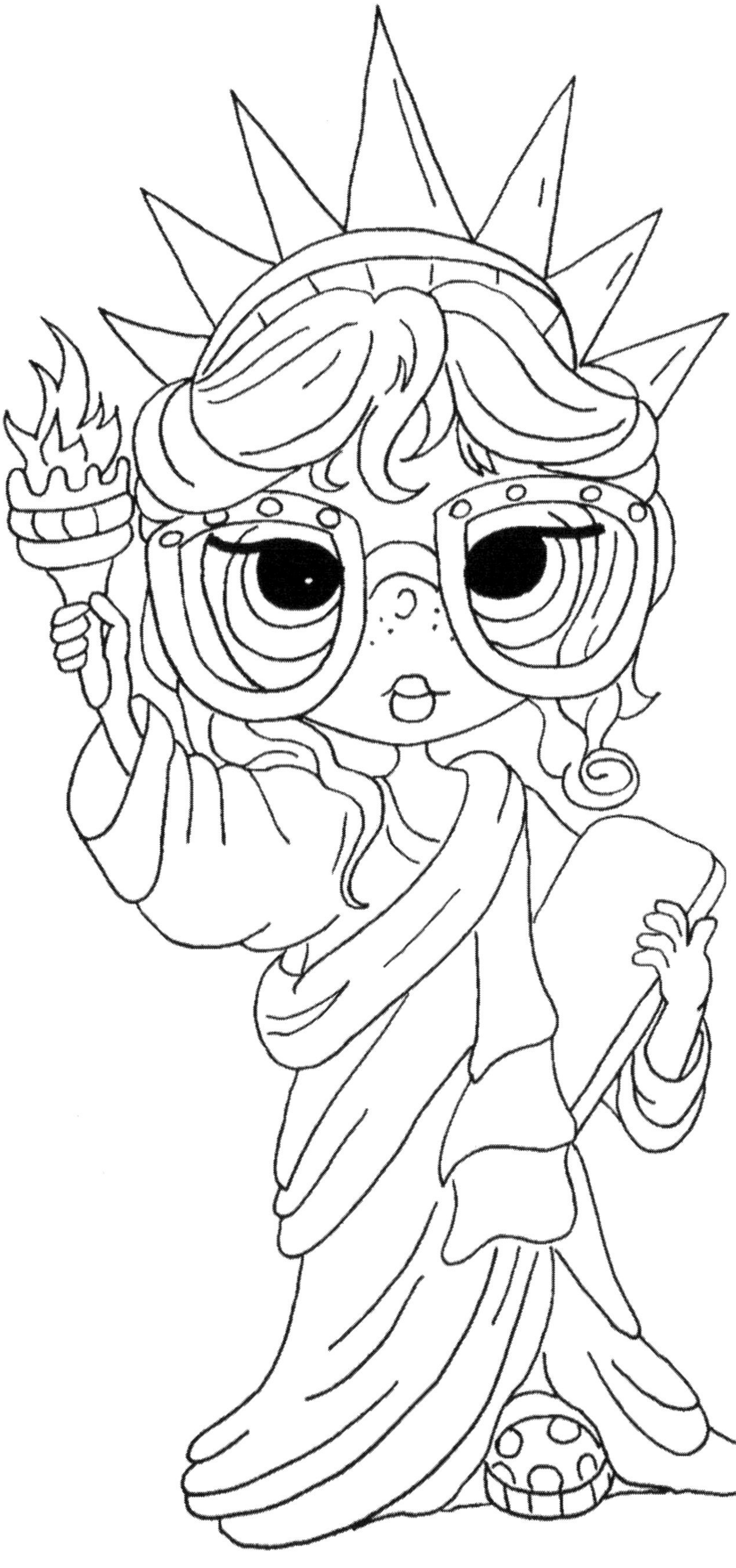

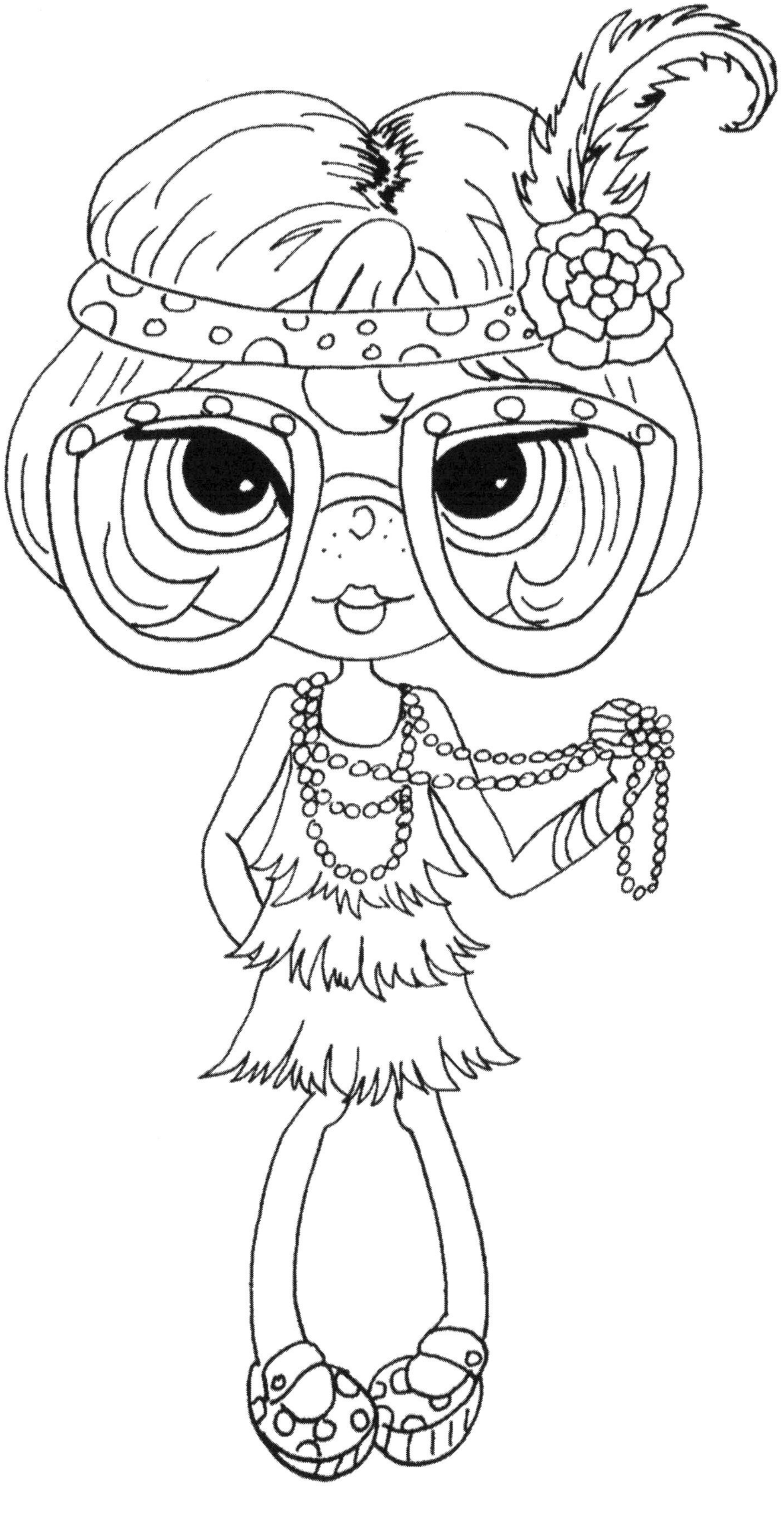

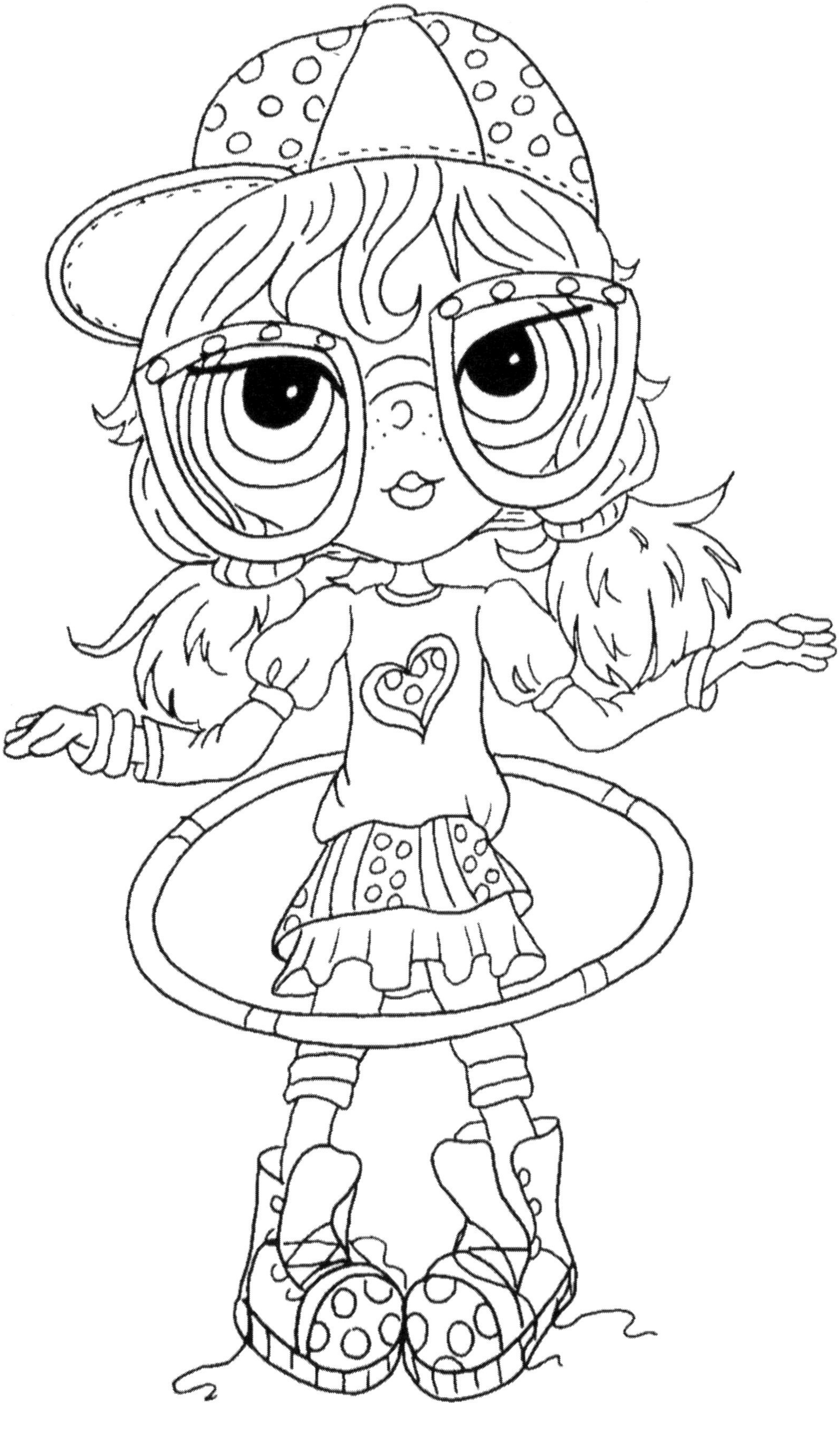

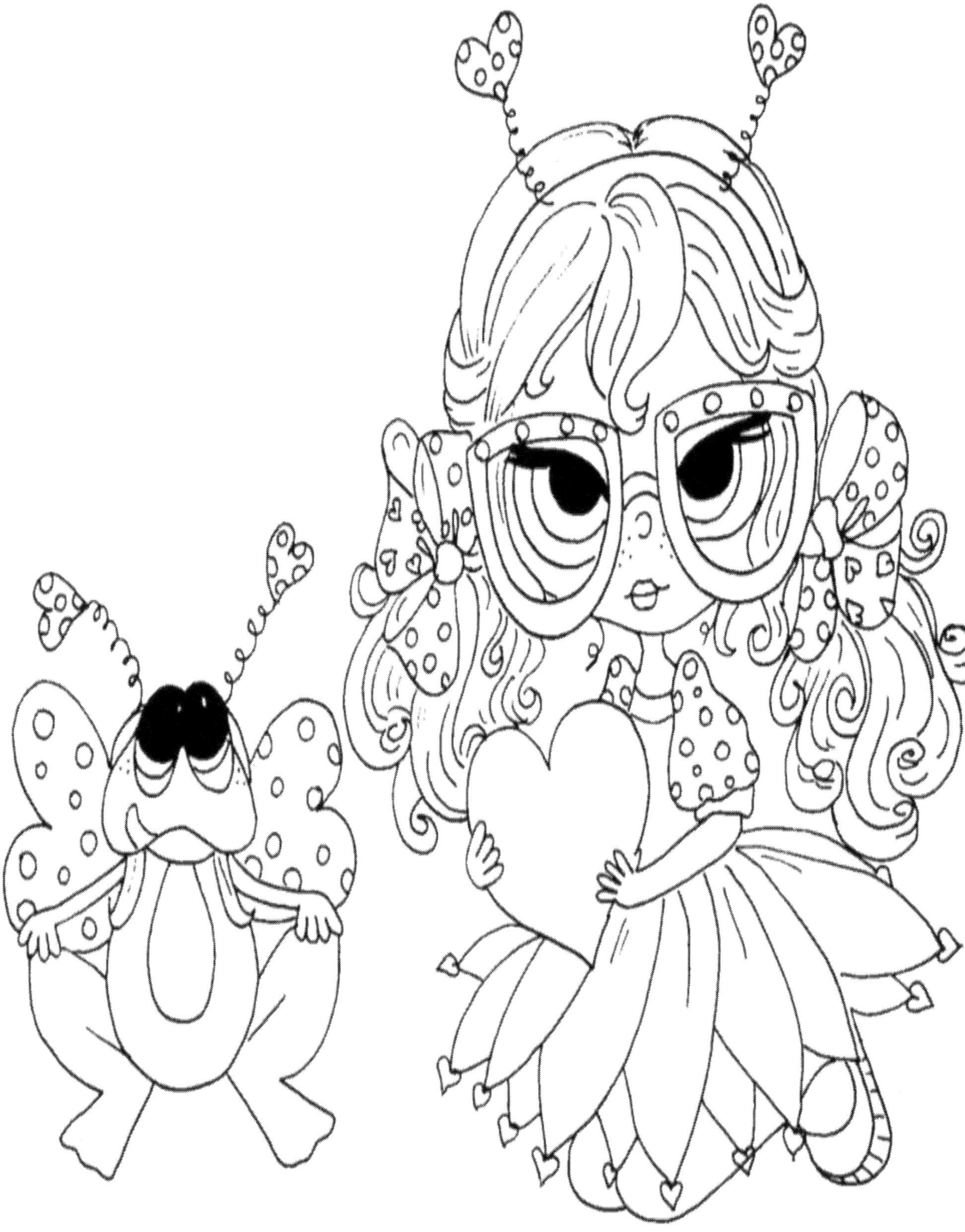

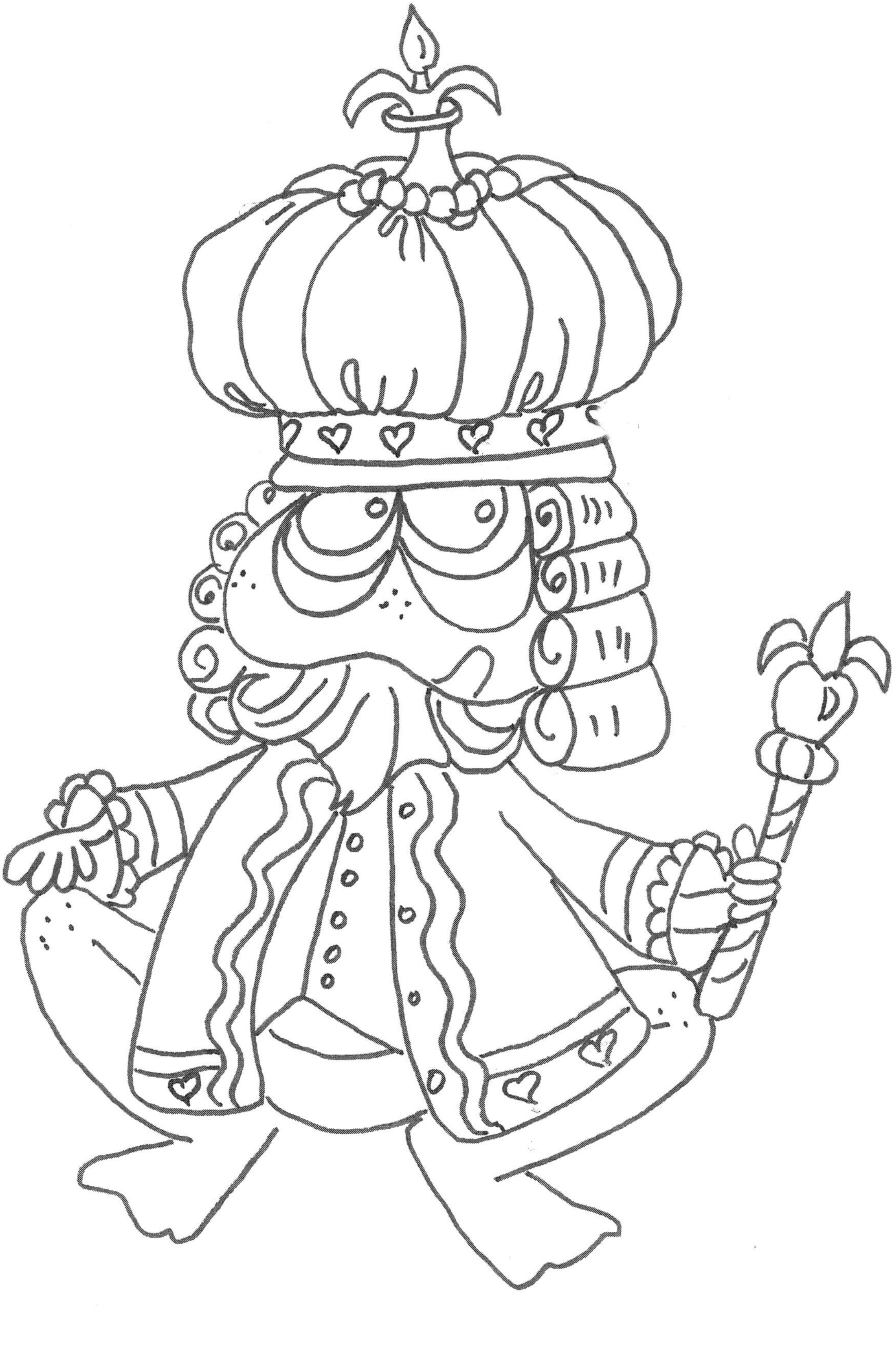

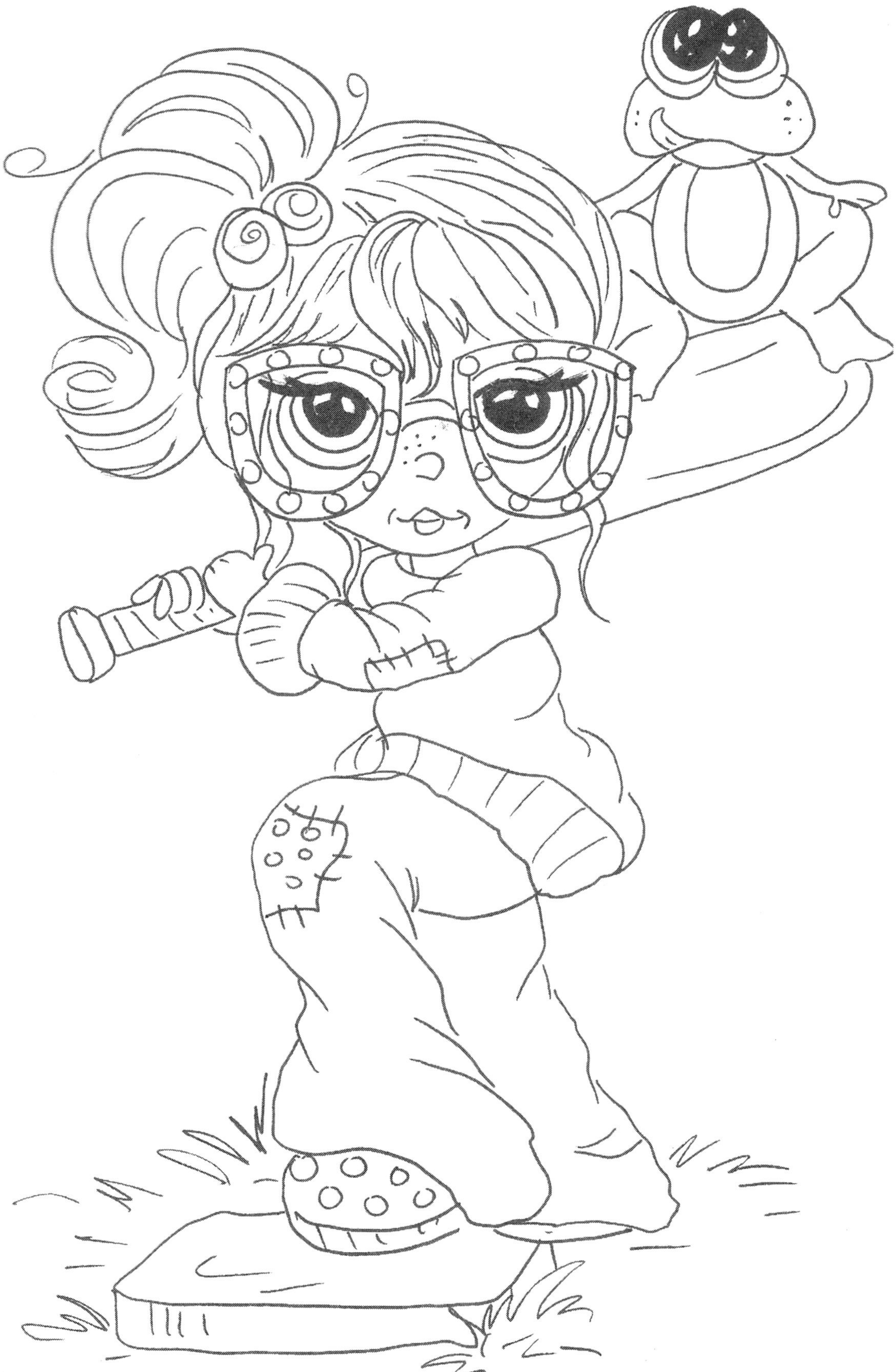

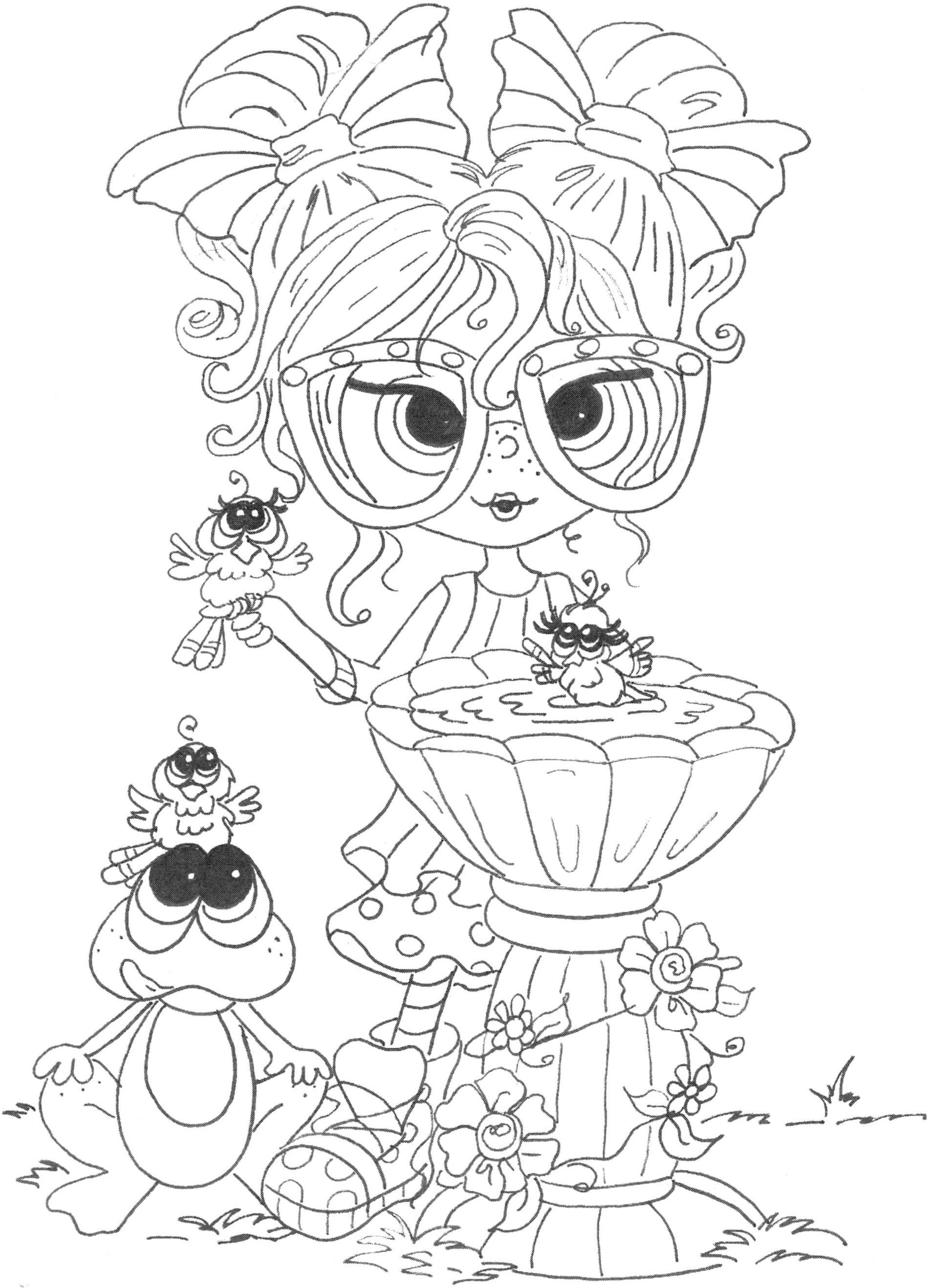

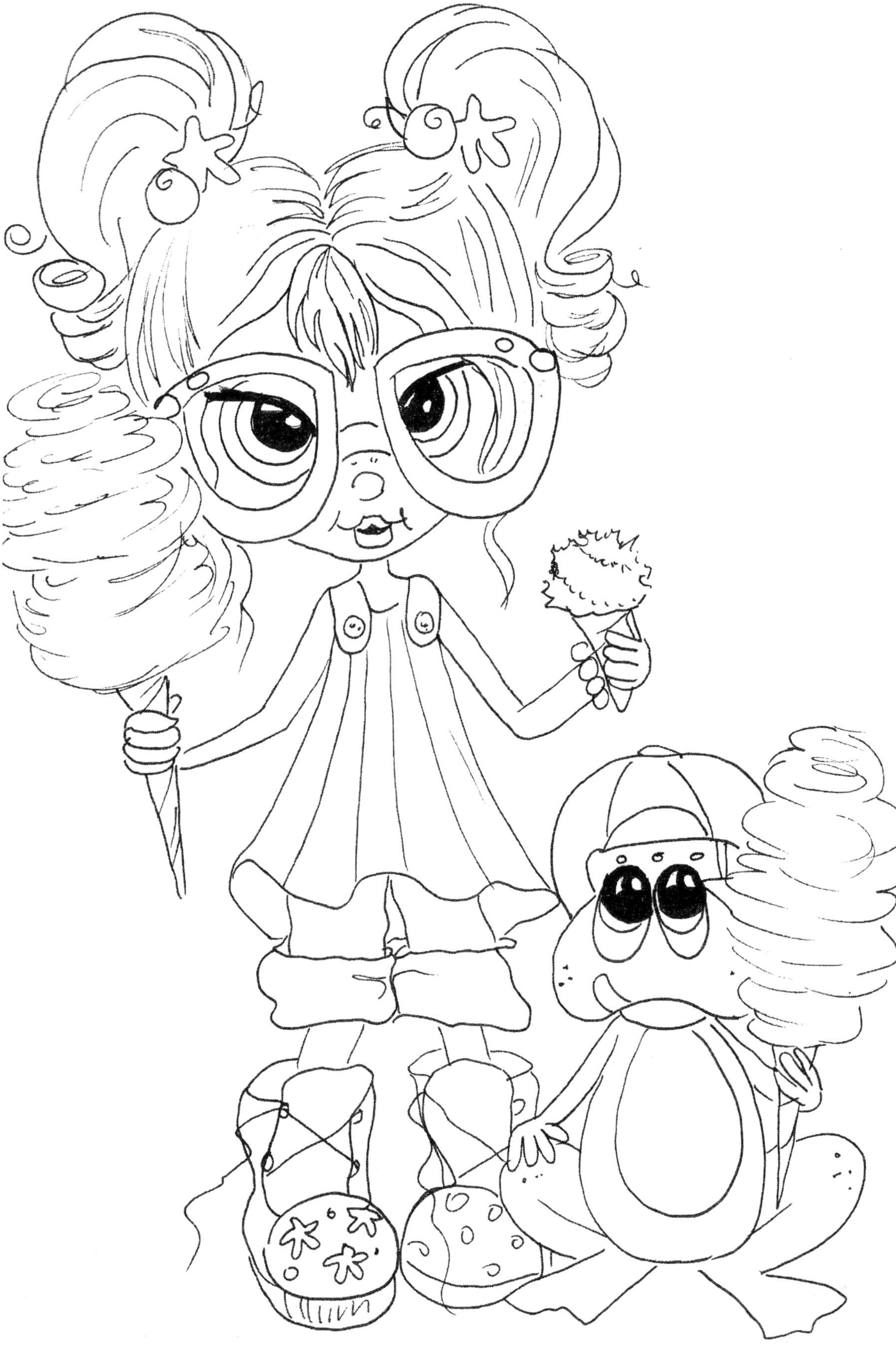

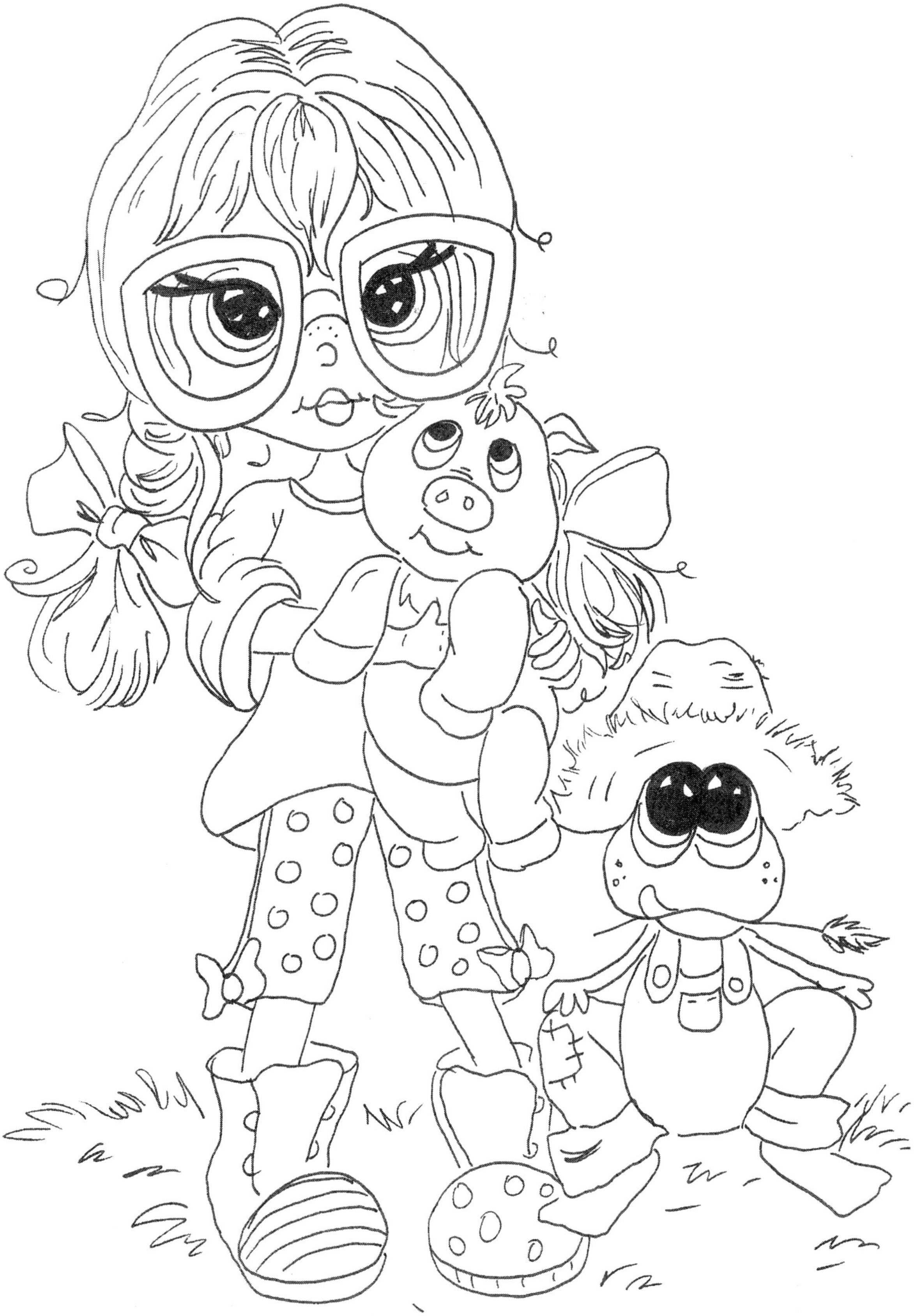

61645365R10042

Made in the USA
San Bernardino, CA
15 December 2017